SOLOMON'S
SUCCESS

SOLOMON'S SUCCESS

FOUR ESSENTIAL KEYS TO LEADERSHIP

kenneth l. samuel

WIPF & STOCK · Eugene, Oregon

To my daughter,

K E N D A L L E ,

and to the present and future generations

of enlightened leaders.

Wipf and Stock Publishers
199 W 8th Ave, Suite 3
Eugene, OR 97401

Solomon's Success
Four Essential Keys to Leadership
By Samuel, Kenneth
Copyright©2006 Pilgrim Press
ISBN 13: 978-1-60899-185-3
Publication date 11/12/2009
Previously published by Pilgrim Press, 2006

contents

introduction

I am an ardent student of biography. I am especially fascinated by the biographies of great "movers and shakers"—persons who have made themselves available to God in exceptional ways to change, redirect, challenge, and transform human society for the advancement of humankind. I am drawn to the biographies of people who are not just famous, but faithful; people who are not just popular, but principled and profound. It amazes me how God works through the foibles and fractures of human personalities to accomplish supernal goals. I am astounded at how God elects to deposit so much heavenly "treasure in earthen vessels" (2 Cor. 4:7) in order to manifest the glory of God's power to redeem and to liberate within the context of human weakness.

History itself is a record of how God uses conflicted human personalities as catalysts for the emergence of extraordinary sociopolitical movements. The Bible is a rich chronicle of faithful personalities who were forged and destined by God to move the structures of human society to higher dimensions of love, life, and enlightenment. Among the many movers and shakers who color the pages of Scripture, there is one who has remained pertinent to our understanding of leadership for over three hundred years.

His name is Solomon—the third king of Israel and the second son born to King David and the beautiful Bathsheba. Of all the monarchs who have ever reigned over a people,

Solomon and his father, David, are among the most revered and respected. In fact, in 1 Kings 3:12, God declares of Solomon, "I now do according to your word. Indeed I give you a wise and discerning mind; no one like you has been before you and no one like you shall arise after you." To this very day, Jews and Judeo-Christians in Israel and throughout the world are still recollecting and reminiscing about the golden glory days of Israel, under the reign of King Solomon. Born in 848 B.C.E. Solomon died at age fifty-two in 796 B.C.E., having ruled as king for forty years. These were the best years in all of Israel's history. The Bible relates that kings and officials from all over the world came to hear Solomon's wisdom, which included not only his understanding of the Torah, but his insights of science and human nature. His fame spread through all the surrounding nations. He composed 3,000 parables and 1,005 poems. He discoursed about trees, from cedars of Lebanon to the hyssop that grows from the wall. He also discoursed about animals, birds, creeping things, and fish. Men of all nations came to hear Solomon's wisdom as did all the kings of the earth who had heard of his wisdom (1 Kgs 5:11–14).

The crowning achievement of Solomon's reign was the building of the Temple in Jerusalem to serve as a permanent place for the Levites to house the Ark of the Covenant, containing the Ten Commandments, as well as performance of their other duties. King David had brought the Ark of the Covenant up to Jerusalem's Mount Moriah—"the gate of heaven"—but because he had been a warrior who had blood on his hands, he was not permitted by God to erect the Temple. The monumental task of building the Temple fell to David's son, Solomon. The Bible devotes several chapters to the construction of this most important building in the nation of Israel—the consecrated place of communion between the Jewish people and God. This magnificent structure, which took seven years to build, was entirely overlaid with gold both inside and outside, including the floors and doors. Additionally, there were bronze structures such as columns, a huge immersion tank, and several exquisite basins and carvings. The erection of Solomon's Temple signaled the pinnacle of Jewish history. All twelve tribes of the nation were united as one, unprecedented domestic prosperity was evidenced, and Israel enjoyed peace on all its borders.

The first two decades of Solomon's forty-year reign were certainly the best. In his later years, Solomon allowed his many wives (seven hundred wives and three hundred concubines) of foreign descent to establish idol worship within the nation. Idol worship in Israel, coupled with Solomon's inclinations to build temples and palaces in order to accommodate the wishes of his wives, brought upon the Israelites heavy taxation, coerced labor, and eventually a civil war that resulted in a divided realm. The military and political alliances that motivated Solomon's marriages to foreigners and that had helped to stabilize the region eventually gave way to the wanton recklessness of imperial opulence and greed.

Notwithstanding the spiritual and political demise of his later years, however, Solomon still stands as a pertinent model for leadership in the twenty-first century. Israel achieved its greatest territorial holdings in history during the reign of King Solomon. It included far more than the traditional Dan to Beersheba of the lands west of the Jordan River. Solomon's realm also included a vast region east of the river in what is today the nation of Jordan, and deep into the northeast, reaching far beyond the Golan Heights all the way to the Euphrates River. Solomon not only transformed a former nation of slaves and nomads into one of the most powerful nations in the Middle East, he also transformed the cultural, economic, and political landscape of the entire region. Israel and the Middle East have not since known the magnitude of peace and prosperity once experienced under the reign of Solomon. These are compelling reasons to look again at the leadership legacy of King Solomon and ascertain what lessons he provides for those of us who face twenty-first-century challenges of leadership.

Why is it that Solomon has spanned the centuries as such a noteworthy icon of wisdom and wealth? What do the life and legacy of Solomon have to say to persons of our day who are seeking to be faithful in their various vocations of servant-leadership? What are the keys to Solomon's enduring success? These are the questions that this book endeavors to address. It is my hope that the answers will not only inform us, but inspire us toward broader visions of God's realm. And I hope that this book will provide some practical insights that will enable us to become more effective in working to advance divine purposes in human society.

This is by no means an extensive or exhaustive study of the life of Solomon. I have purposefully written in broad strokes and have sought to arrange my ideas around four pivotal aspects of Solomon's character and performance as a leader. I trust that my succinctness will not do serious damage to the subject matter, but will allow us greater facility in connecting with the power and the possibilities presented through Solomon's leadership. It is my prayer that this concise consideration of the leadership of Solomon will help us to critically evaluate our own leadership performance in the context of our contemporary challenges and, as a result, make ourselves more available to be used by God for progressive social change both within and outside of Christendom.

1

THE FIRST KEY: WISDOM

---

1 Kings 3:4–13 (NIV)

4 The king went to Gibeon to offer sacrifices, for that was the most important high place, and Solomon offered a thousand burnt offerings on that altar.

5 At Gibeon God appeared to Solomon during the night in a dream, and God said, "Ask for whatever you want me to give you."

6 Solomon answered, "You have shown great kindness to your servant, my father David, because he was faithful to you and righteous and upright in heart. You have continued this great kindness to him and have given him a son to sit on his throne this very day.

7 Now, O my Sovereign God, you have made your servant king in place of my father David. But I am only a little child and do not know how to carry out my duties.

8 Your servant is here among the people you have chosen, a great people, too numerous to count or number.

9 So give your servant a discerning heart to govern your people and to distinguish between right and wrong. For who is able to govern this great people of yours?"

10 God was pleased that Solomon had asked for this.

11 So God said to him, "Since you have asked for this and not for long life or wealth for yourself, nor have asked for the death of your enemies but for discernment in administering justice,

12   I will do what you have asked. I will give you a wise and discerning heart, so that there will never have been anyone like you, nor will there ever be.

13   Moreover, I will give you what you have not asked for—both riches and honor—so that in your lifetime you will have no equal among kings."

THE WISDOM TO GIVE IN ORDER TO RECEIVE

The first key to Solomon's success is wisdom. In 1 Kings 3:4, we find the young King Solomon in a place called Gibeon, which was located six miles northwest of Jerusalem. In that place, Solomon offers God a thousand burnt offerings. A burnt offering, as compared to other sacrificial offerings, was an offering that had to be completely burned on the altar. None of the animals offered as a burnt offering could be eaten by the worshipers or the priests, as was the case with other sacrificial offerings.

A burnt offering had to be offered as a gift to God in its entirety; it had to be completely consumed by the fire on the altar. Solomon offered a thousand burnt offerings to God at Gibeon—a substantial gift indeed! If Solomon offered bulls at an estimated cost of five hundred dollars each in our currency, the cost of his thousand burnt offerings would have been approximately five hundred thousand dollars. Such an offering would have been feasible for a person of his stature and means. If Solomon had offered goats or rams at an estimated cost of one hundred dollars each, the cost of a thousand burnt offerings would have been at least one hundred thousand dollars, not counting the costs of oil and wood to burn the sacrifice—another quite substantial amount. The point here is that what Solomon offered to God cost him something substantial. And in offering to

God that which cost him something substantial, Solomon actually placed himself in position to receive something substantial from God. Substantial gifts do not come without substantial costs. God gives much to those who evidence a willingness to give generously from that which they have been blessed to receive.

The wisdom of Solomon is first evidenced in the text by Solomon's willingness to offer God something substantial. Most often, the measure of what we desire to receive from God is not commensurate with the measure of what we are willing to give back to God in terms of our time, treasure, and service to others. Many believers are under the mistaken impression that we can come to God empty handed, empty headed, and empty hearted and expect to receive from God substantial blessings and benefits. But Jesus teaches us in Luke 6:38 that what we receive from God is directly proportionate to what we are willing to give: "Give and it will be given to you. A good measure, pressed down, shaken together, running over, will be put into your lap; for the measure you give will be the measure you get back."

Every great leader and every faithful disciple must be willing to pay a high cost. The sacrifices of time, energy, and the pursuit of personal pleasures, which are required for effective leadership, are substantially high. How much of our personal perks, privileges, and prizes are we really willing to sacrifice so we can be used by God? What portion/percentage of our personal wealth have we consecrated exclusively to the glory of God? How much of the quality time that we spend with family, with friends, and in pursuit of personal passions are we willing to sacrifice in order to make ourselves more available for leadership preparation and service? How much personal comfort and security are we willing to forgo in order to publicly proclaim our ultimate devotion to God?

Salvation is free, but it's certainly not cheap. Salvation comes to us at a great cost. The cost required heaven to surrender its very best, caused angels to stand in awe, and grieved the very heart of God. Solomon's offering at Gibeon evidenced his willingness to make substantial sacrifices to God. And in so doing, Solomon placed himself in position to receive substantial blessings from God. How much are we willing to sacrifice for the realm? How much are we willing to give in order to receive?

Whenever we give an offering to God, we are really making a statement about our love and appreciation for God. We often say, "It's not the gift, but the thought that counts." But try offering a cheap gift to a loved one on an occasion when your gift should reflect your gratitude. Try talking about "the thought that counts" as you present a cheap gift to a loved one who knows what you are able to afford. That song just won't sing. The more we love someone, the more we want to offer gifts that speak substantially of our love and appreciation for that person. Likewise, our gifts to God should reflect our love and gratitude for God. Any gift of time, talent, or treasure we offer God that is less substantial than the best that we are able to give God is insulting and inappropriate. No wonder Solomon's father, David, said in 2 Samuel 24:24: "I will not offer burnt offerings to my Sovereign God that cost me nothing."

Solomon's offering to God at Gibeon cost him something substantial. He gave to God something substantial, and thereby placed himself in position to receive from God something substantial as well. We never lose anything when we give God our best. Have you ever noticed that people who are always giving always have something to give? On the other hand, those who give little or nothing seem to be in chronic complaint about their deficits. We can only stand to gain as we give freely, cheerfully, and substantially to the glory of God. While Solomon was in Gibeon giving a substantial offering to God, God showed up with a substantial offer for Solomon. At Gibeon, God appeared to Solomon in a dream—a vision, if you please. In the vision, God said to Solomon: "Ask me for whatever you want me to give you."

THE WISDOM OF KNOWING HOW TO HANDLE GOD'S ABUNDANCE

Solomon's life teaches us that certain blessings only come to us as we make ourselves and our resources available to be a blessing. While Solomon was making a substantial offering to God, God showed up and made him a substantial offer. In the process of our thanking God for what we have, God shows up to supply what we need. In the process of our giving God the best we've got, God shows up to add more to us. In the process of our expressing our gratitude to God for what we have received, God shows up to give us more for which we can be grateful. While Solomon was offering substantial sacrifices to God at Gibeon, God showed up and said to him: "Ask me for whatever you want me to give you." It's as if God offers Solomon a blank check in response to the trustworthiness of Solomon's stewardship.

Now, the question is what will Solomon do with a blank check endorsed by God? How will Solomon respond to the limitless possibilities of such an extravagant offer? Will Solomon be able to handle the astounding generosity of God's gratuitous favor? These are important questions, because not many of us can handle abundance and unlimited possibilities very well. In fact, history would indicate that we seem capable of handling scarcity much better than we are able to handle prosperity. We know how to struggle to put food on our tables, and how to still say grace over pork and beans and light bread, but can we sit down to prime rib, lobster, caviar, and Cristal and still not forget that humankind does not live by bread alone?

We know how to pray and struggle to get through school and pay tuition, but can we stand proudly with graduation robes on our backs, tassels on our heads, stripes on our sleeves, and degrees in our hands and not forget that the fear or reverence of God is the beginning of knowledge? We know how to survive in slums and ghettoes and still remember that we are God's temples, but can we live in eclectic subdivisions and gentrified condominiums and still not forget that God is our dwelling place from generation to generation? We know how to wear hand-me-downs and still act like we are somebody, but can we wear Parisian, Joseph A. Bank, St. John, Fubu, and Phat Pharm without forgetting to put on the whole armor of God? We know how to ride in the back of the bus and still bless God, but can we drive the bus or own the bus and drive a Mercedes, Lexus, or SUV and still remember that we walk by faith and not by sight? We know how to have church without air conditioning and still shout for joy, but can we sit up in climate controlled edifices without being too cool, too cold, too conceited, too cute, too cranky, and too cocky to say "Thank you, Jesus!?" History reveals our capacity to handle scarcity much better than abundance.

Solomon was put to the test. God said to him, "Ask me for whatever you want me to give you." Solomon could have choked on the amazing grandeur of God's limitless offer. Or he could have rushed to seize benefits for his own self-aggrandizement by requesting heaven's resources to secure his own personal gain. Much of our prayers and petitions to God are directed expressly and exclusively to these ends. So much of popular religion these days is structured around the motif of personal prosperity and private gain. So much of popular religion today is nothing more than a pious sanctification of materialism.

Solomon could have sought to secure his own personal prosperity via the limitless possibilities of God's amazing offer. Instead, however, Solomon was wise enough to look beyond his personal aggrandizement to embrace his divine purpose. In so doing, Solomon proved that at this particular juncture in his life, he could handle the amazing abundance of God's bountiful blessings.

THE WISDOM TO ACKNOWLEDGE ONE'S HISTORY

Before Solomon asked God for anything, Solomon was wise enough to be mindful of what God had already provided for him. Solomon begins his response to God's amazing offer by expressing appreciation to God for his history. In 1 Kings 3:6, Solomon says: "You have shown great and steadfast love to your servant my father David, because he walked before you in faithfulness, in righteousness, and in uprightness of heart toward you; and you have kept for him this great and steadfast love, and have given him a son to sit on his throne today."

Here, Solomon teaches us the wisdom of appreciating what God has already done in our history as we seek God's favor for our present and future. Too many times we petition God for present and future blessings with a lack of appreciation for what God has already provided.

We sometimes act as if every prayer we pray is from ground zero, and that we have nothing for which we can be grateful. In our desires to get more from God, we are often unmindful and unthankful for what God has already provided. Truthfully, God's goodness toward us is longstanding. God has been opening doors and making ways for us long before we ever discovered our present needs and desires. Every current petition we bring before God should be accompanied by appreciation and praise for what God has already provided. In fact, it is our acute awareness of what God has already done for us that gives us the confidence to believe that God's grace is still sufficient to supply all of our current needs. In "Amazing Grace," lyricist John Newton in 1779 intoned:

> Through many dangers, toils and snares I have already come;
> 'Tis grace hath brought me safe thus far, and grace will lead me home.

Facing the violent and virulent systems of racial oppression that plagued his time, Dr. Martin Luther King Jr. was able to draw courage from the faithful struggles of his fore-parents. In appreciation for what God had done through his history, Dr. King was emboldened to speak hope to the dismal circumstances of his present:

> If the inexpressible cruelties of slavery could not stop us, the opposition we now face will surely fail; because the sacred heritage of our nation and the eternal will of God are embodied in our echoing demands.[1]

The wisdom of Solomon teaches us to be appreciative for the favor of God evidenced throughout our history, and, in particular, Solomon's wisdom teaches us to be especially grateful for our parents. In 1 Kings 3:6, Solomon say to God, "You have shown great and steadfast love to your servant my father David, because he walked in faithfulness, in righteousness, and in uprightness." Without accusing Solomon of promoting a revisionist view of history concerning his father, those of us who are familiar with the life and exploits of King David in the Old Testament would agree that God's kindness to him was not always in response to his faithful obedience. Like all of us, David enjoyed the favor of God despite his many transgressions. Solomon's wisdom teaches us that parents don't have to be perfect in order to be good parents. Just as God worked through the imperfections and inconsistencies of David to deliver Solomon, God continues to work through the imperfections and inconsistencies of parents to deliver sons and daughters today.

Most people did not enjoy the luxury of growing up in a "Huxtable home." All of us are products of some form of family dysfunction—some, no doubt, more damaging than others. Solomon was no exception. The union between David and Solomon's mother, Bathsheba, was executed in a whirlwind of lust and deceit that eventually led to murder (see 2 Sam. 11). Nonetheless, God worked through the dysfunctions of David to deliver the throne of Israel to his son, Solomon. It is possible to curse our parents while we simultaneously replicate their mistakes and perpetuate their dysfunctions. It is far wiser to be conscious of our parents' human flaws, and then be careful not to replicate their indiscretions.

We can learn how to be more compassionate and sensitive to the young and the vulnerable even if we lived with abusive parents. We can learn how to be less controlling and domineering of the lives of people we love even if we lived with obsessive parents. We can learn how to be honest and open in building relationships even if we have manipulative relatives. We can learn how to allow everyone the right of self-expression, and how to love people for who they are even if we have self-righteous, judgmental family members. What we learn from the dysfunctions of our family history can strengthen and brighten the way for present and future generations. God can turn the laments of our past into enlightenment for our present and future. God extracted hope from David's checkered past and rested it upon his son, Solomon.

Solomon's wisdom reminds us to be thankful for our history as we assess our needs for the present and future. It is virtually impossible for us to have a clear vision for our present and future without a clear understanding and appreciation of our past. Malcolm X said that "a people's history is a people's memory." Without memory we are all clueless and unable to connect the dots that move us from where we are to where God is leading us. A songwriter has said: "As I look back over my life, and I think things over, I can truly say that I've been blessed, I've got a testimony!"[2] Without testimonies from the past, we will surely fail our tests in the present.

THE WISDOM TO APPRECIATE ONE'S OPPORTUNITY

In addition to being grateful for our history, we are also taught by Solomon to be appreciative for our present opportunities. In 1 Kings 3:7 Solomon says: "And now, O my Sovereign God, you have made your servant king in place of my father David."

Here the wisdom of Solomon speaks to us about the need to be conscious of the present opportunities and possibilities that God places before each of us. Are we cognizant of the opportunities God has currently laid before us? There are opportunities for personal and professional growth, opportunities for higher learning, opportunities to become more focused in the pursuit of a desired goal, opportunities to learn from and to correct past mistakes and failures, opportunities to read and reflect more in order to develop our critical thinking capacities, opportunities to make our time and our resources more available for the advancement of God's realm through volunteerism or involvement in church ministry.

Opportunities for service, discovery, enrichment, and advancement are embedded in every day that we are allowed to live, move, and have our being At the outset of his reign as ruler of Israel, Solomon understood the golden opportunity that God had placed before him. His ascension to the throne of Israel signaled a monumental era of transition—both for himself and for his nation. In the midst of the changes and challenges involved in the transition of rulers, Solomon saw opportunity. We can surmise that Solomon viewed his opportunities as king to be much greater than any obstacles he faced. Just imagine what might happen . . . just imagine what could happen if, in our hearts and minds, we were to give our opportunities priority over our obstacles. Imagine what could happen if we were to see in every change and challenge of our lives the opportunity for growth, service, and development.

Imagine facing the challenges of marriage, mindful of the opportunity it affords us to develop a love which enables us to believe all things, hope all things and endure all things (1 Cor. 13). Imagine facing the transitions of a divorce, mindful of the opportunity it provides for us to learn how to assess and forgive ourselves as well as the person from whom we are being separated. Imagine embracing a lucrative employment or a profitable windfall, mindful of the opportunity that money provides to become more responsible for the empowerment and well-being of the less fortunate—those whom Jesus called "the least of these." Imagine facing the challenges of a financial deficit, mindful of the opportunity it provides to become more efficient and less wanton as stewards of God's resources.

Just imagine what might happen . . . what could happen, if we began each of our days with an appreciation for our God-given opportunities instead of a fixation on our obstacles and challenges. In the midst of the tremendous challenges of his transition to the throne, Solomon was mindful of his very special opportunities.

THE WISDOM TO ADMIT ONE'S INADEQUACY

Before Solomon asked God for anything, Solomon considered the opportunity he had been given as successor to the throne of his father David. In lieu of his awesome opportunity, however, Solomon was honest enough to admit his own inadequacy: "I am only a little child and do not know how to carry out my duties" (1 Kings 3:7 NIV). Solomon was not literally a little child, but he was very young (probably in his teens) and he had been blessed with the awesome opportunity and responsibility to lead the nation of Israel. Solomon sincerely wished to take full advantage of the opportunity bequeathed upon him by God, but he was wise enough not to make the mistake of confusing his position of leadership with his capacity to lead.

The position or place of leadership is one thing; the capacity or ability to lead is quite another. Sitting in the driver's seat as the designated driver is one thing; knowing how to drive and where to drive is another. Solomon was in a definite position of leadership. As ruler of Israel, he occupied the highest political office in the land. Yet his high position did not preclude him from exercising the humility he needed to admit that he could not accomplish his awesome assignment without divine direction.

Strong leaders are the first to admit what they don't know. Strong leaders are the first to recognize their inadequacies and solicit direction from God and assistance from others. Solomon was wise enough and honest enough to say: "God, I don't know how to do what you have already given me the responsibility to do."

Overconfidence in one's own abilities can breed a certain incompetence in leadership. Whenever we are called to lead people, we must deal with a host of human variables. These variables are as mysterious and unpredictable as human life itself. Sometimes our egos will not allow us to be honest about our own inadequacies. Sometimes we assume that a position, a title, or a designation itself is all that is required to lead. The truth is that no one is completely competent in himself or herself to accomplish the tasks of leading people. Leadership always requires more than the abilities we can provide in and of ourselves. God gives leadership assignments that require us to seek God for what we do not have and to trust God for what we cannot do in and of ourselves. God gives leadership assignments that require us to listen and learn from others. Every faithful leader ought to be keenly and constantly aware of his or her inadequacies in the face of God's awesome assignment to lead people.

There is great wisdom in the realization of one's own limitations, and, like Solomon, each of us must be honest enough and wise enough to admit them. Like Solomon, parents have to be honest enough to admit, "I don't know," and thereby open themselves to learning something new from their own children. Like Solomon, professionals have to be honest enough to admit, "I don't know," and thereby open up clearer lines of communication and collaboration with their coworkers and their clients. Like Solomon, elected officials have to be honest enough to admit, "I don't know," and govern with a keen sense of humility. Like Solomon, Christians have to be honest enough to admit, "I don't know," and thereby open their hearts and minds to new directives and insights from the God, who is still speaking.

Solomon was honest enough to admit, "I don't know." In the context, this was a rather startling admission. Monarchs were not known to acknowledge their inadequacies. The same can be said for persons of high position in our society today. A wise person has said that power does not necessarily corrupt; power reveals. Power does not necessarily engender arrogance; it reveals arrogance. For the past several years, America has been embroiled in a bitter conflict in Iraq. This conflict has claimed the lives of over two thousand American troops and tens of thousands of Iraqi citizens. More than a few American citizens have misgivings about the war in Iraq, which stem from a wide perception that the justifications given for the war are invalid. No one argues against the need for decisiveness in a commander-in-chief, but a decision to go to war must be made with utmost care. It is the cockiness and imperial air of those who led us into war that is most disturbing.

A foreign policy built upon blind retaliation and unilateralism will prove to be inadequate in securing the peace of our nation and the world. Those who sit in positions of high political power have much to learn from the wisdom, the humility, and the honesty of Solomon. An honest admission of what we don't know is not a sign of weakness. On the contrary, it opens the door to greater insight and understanding for prudent direction in our decision making. There are many questions to which the answer, "I or we don't know," would be the wisest and most honest answer. Was there sufficient evidence to justify the invasion and occupation of Iraq? At the very least, the only honest answer would be, "We don't know."

Does the United States have a viable exit strategy out of Iraq? Somebody in high authority ought to be honest enough to say, "I don't know."

Given the growing disdain for the United States throughout the Muslim world, will the U.S. occupation of Iraq really help to foster democracy in the Middle East? Somebody in high authority ought to be honest enough to say, "I don't know."

Was George W. Bush fairly elected by the majority of eligible voters who cast their ballot in the presidential election of 2000? Many of us think we already know the answer to this question, but to help the nation heal from that regrettable episode, somebody in the White House should at least admit, "I don't know," especially since hundreds of thousands of likely Democratic votes were discarded and/or miscounted.

So much of our public, personal, and private lives could be helped by the honest admission of "I don't know." Our individual and institutional lives would be much better if we confessed our inadequacies. Such a confession would surely invite greater dialogue among us and greater intervention from God. When Solomon admitted his inadequacy in light of his awesome opportunity, he opened himself and his endeavors to the eternal dimensions of divine direction and divine resources. He and his nation benefited immeasurably because of his honest admission.

THE WISDOM TO CELEBRATE THE GREATNESS OF OTHERS

Solomon's response to God's offer of a "blank check" did not end with the acknowledgement of his history, the appreciation of his opportunity, and the admission of his inadequacy. Solomon went on to acknowledge and to celebrate the greatness of the people of his community. Solomon said to God, "Your servant is here among the people you have chosen, a great people, too numerous to count or number" (1 Kgs 3:8 NIV).

Even while seated at the pinnacle of power and prestige in Israel, Solomon was not so blinded by his own prominence that he could not see the greatness of the people around him. The greatness of Israel was not defined by their numbers alone. Israel was a great nation because God had chosen it to express God's love and reconciliation to all people's of the world. It is not common for a person who is especially gifted or endowed to have the circumspect insight to recognize the giftedness and special endowments of others.

We're each tempted to become the centers of our own universe, and the more endowed we are, the more self-centered our universe becomes. It is possible to become so buoyed by the prominence of one's own giftedness that one becomes virtually oblivious to any reflections of greatness in anyone else. It is possible for a church or a denomination to become so caught up in its own blessed anointing that it cannot see the truth and the power of God revealed in any diverse religious expression.

It is possible for a nation to become so fixated by the pride of its own heritage that national pride becomes a justification for nationalistic supremacy. Persons and peoples who are especially blessed and gifted must be careful to avoid the temptations of narcissism on every level. Truly great people are able to recognize and to celebrate greatness in somebody other than themselves.

In the eyes of Egypt and the other superpowers of the world during Solomon's era, the children of Abraham may not have been counted as a great people. But Solomon had the insight to see greatness among a people who had not yet even reached their full potential as a nation. He saw greatness in a people who had little or no recognition among the prominent nations of his day. The ability to see greatness among classes of people who have historically been oppressed and discounted is a very precious and rare insight in any community.

In 2005, Oprah Winfrey evidenced this precious insight when she hosted a luncheon at her California estate to honor the greatness of twenty-five trail-blazing African American women. Those phenomenal women were: Maya Angelou, Shirley Caesar, Diahann Carroll, Elizabeth Catlett, Ruby Dee, Katherine Dunham, Roberta Flack, Aretha Franklin, Nikki Giovanni, Dorothy Height, Lena Horne, Coretta Scott King, Gladys Knight, Patti LaBelle, Toni Morrison, Rosa Parks, Leontyne Price, Della Reese, Diana Ross, Naomi Sims, Tina Turner, Cicely Tyson, Alice Walker, Dionne Warwick, and Nancy Wilson.

According to Oprah, "these women broke barriers through the sheer force of their excellence, and they continue to inspire and pave the way for countless others behind them."

In a real sense, Oprah's "Legends Luncheon" was not only a tribute to the greatness of African American woman who have made it to the top of their professions. It also served as a catalyst to recognize and beckon the potential for greatness that lies in the hearts of all women—especially black women. And more so for black women who have had to exercise extraordinary creative genius in order to overcome the preclusions of historical and systemic racial/gender impediments. The luncheon was designed not just to honor the "Legends," but to also inspire the "young'uns"—those who have yet to realize their full potential. Oprah used her prominent platform as "America's Girlfriend" to give the luncheon/celebration the national attention it deserved. She motivated the American nation to pay attention and to pay tribute to the very class of people it had disrespected and denied for centuries. For black women, the move from slave mammies to international cultural icons has by no means been easy, and Oprah's salute to these phenomenal women of an oppressed lineage, gave occasion for all Americans to pause and salute them as well.

Solomon was at the top of his game, as Oprah is now. Both Solomon and Oprah could have easily preoccupied themselves with the perks and privileges of their own preeminence. Instead, they both chose to look around themselves and recognize the greatness of others. This is a true sign of wisdom and it is a true sign of great leadership.

To see greatness in the least among us is a rare insight indeed. As leaders in our homes, families, and communities, we must cultivate an ability to perceive greatness in unlikely persons and places. And we must develop a willingness to call greatness forth among everyday people in anticipatory celebration. There are more Maya Angelous among us; they just have yet to find their voices. There are more Abraham Lincolns among us; they just have yet to find their cause. There are more James Baldwins among us; they just have yet to write their stories. There are more Muhammad Alis among us; they just have yet to find anything for which to fight. There are more Eleanor Roosevelts among us; they just have yet to realize their potential. There are more Michael Jordans among us; they just have yet to find their team. There are more Stevie Wonders among us; they just have yet to close their eyes and open their minds to inner visions. There are more Martin Luther Kings among us; they just have yet to express their dreams.

Great leaders are able to recognize and call forth greatness in others. Solomon possessed the heart and the wisdom of a great leader. He was able to celebrate greatness in persons over whom he had authority. Only after he had acknowledged his history, appreciated his opportunity, admitted his inadequacy, and celebrated the greatness of others, did Solomon fill in the blank check extended to him by God. Solomon asked God for an understanding heart—a heart of discernment—so that he could govern his people wisely and make critically accurate distinctions between right and wrong.

THE WISDOM OF A DISCERNING HEART

The value of a discerning heart has been lost to many in our contemporary culture. Popular Christian evangelicalism proclaims that the issues of right and wrong are as easy to distinguish as black and white. Consequently, many sincere Christians subscribe to a set of moral absolutes that they believe define and categorize every issue in life for eternity.

The young King Solomon had a much more profound understanding of human life and moral imperatives. He understood how important it would be for him, as a leader, to have the capacity to comprehend the fine nuances of morality; to see beyond the appearance of ethical behavior; and to discern the hidden subtleties of good and evil. Solomon was wise enough to understand that life does not easily fit into neatly divided, well-delineated categories. Life constantly spills over into new and undefined territories. Life constantly takes us to places we have never been and ushers us into experiences that we cannot easily explain. Life often challenges our religious assumptions about what is right and what is wrong. Life often forces us to go to the Scriptures and seek for meanings that are deeper and truer than that which is made apparent by the literal text.

Life defies simplistic answers, and effective leaders must covet and cultivate hearts of discernment; hearts that listen carefully; hearts that think profoundly; hearts that see beyond the superficial; hearts that feel the intangible; and hearts that move according to a much deeper insight than that which is nominally evident. A heart of discernment is the key to a fulfilled life.

DISCERNMENT IN ROMANCE

Hard-heartedness speaks to the inability of an individual to see beyond his/her own interests and comprehend the feelings and interests of another. Hard-heartedness blocks an individual from becoming emotionally, intellectually and spiritually intimate with another person. Countless relationships suffer because of the hard-heartedness of one or both partners. Jesus himself identifies hard-heartedness as the root cause of divorce in Mark 10:2-5. What person in a committed relationship would not value a mate with a heart to look deeply and incisively into his/her passions and interest? Intimacy is the ability to see beyond self into the soul of another. Is this not what we each long for, look for? The ability and the willingness to see into the heart of the persons we love and to whom we respond appropriately is something that is worth far more than money, material, and good looks.

Solomon teaches us that a heart of discernment, which gives us the capacity for intimacy, is not something that is innate to human nature. We are each born with a natural proclivity to beguile ourselves and our loved ones with a fixation on that which is self-gratifying. According to the creation story in Genesis, Adam and Eve ruined the intimacy they shared between themselves and the intimacy they shared with God. They elevated the superficial satisfaction derived from their indulgence of the forbidden tree in the Garden of Eden over their deeper relationship to their Creator.

Because they could not see beyond their own immediate gratification, they lost their innocence with one another and their intimacy with God. Therefore, one of the human consequences of "the fall" in Eden is the natural human tendency to subscribe to that which is superficially gratifying.

A heart of discernment, which enables us to look past our self-aggrandizement in order to secure the relationships with our loved ones, is an essential component of intimacy. The willingness and the capacity to sensitize our hard hearts to the extent that we can look past our self-centeredness and see deeply into the needs and interests of another is the only thing that can sustain our friendships, partnerships, and marriages. Solomon asked for the ability to discern the needs of others.

DISCERNMENT IN BUSINESS

The shifting trends and demands of the marketplace require business people who possess hearts that are perceptive enough to see and anticipate the needs and concerns of consumers. Many businesses have become unprofitable for having made the fatal mistake of placing profits before people. This mistake bespeaks a lack of business insight. Price and profits are not the only things that drive business. Good business people are discerning enough to understand that they are selling image, sentimentality, and customer satisfaction as well as a commodity. The key to good business is a concern for and a connectedness with people. People, not profits, drive business.

Only business leaders with hearts of discernment can serve, shape, and even help to define the needs of the market significantly. At one time, IBM enjoyed the lion's share of the computer industry. But instead of making the needs of the individual consumers its priority, IBM tried to protect its profits by catering to its corporate clients. Bill Gate's perception of the individual consumer's needs allowed him to discover and to help define a whole new market for personal computers. Microsoft has now superceded IBM because it exercised discernment in assessing the needs and concerns of people. Microsoft was born out of a desire to serve people, not just corporations. A heart for the discernment of people's needs not only makes a business profitable, it also makes a business good. Consequently, the American populace must become discerning enough to support businesses that are not only profitable, but morally and socially responsible.

The Wal-Mart Corporation is the largest and most profitable retailer in the world. Its low price guarantee has certainly met a demand in the market, and Wal-Mart has arguably been a significant contributor to the economic revitalization of some depressed communities across the nation. But Wal-Mart's low prices come at a high cost to the company's low wage, nonunion workforce.

At a time when many communities are experiencing the vulnerability and uncertainty of economic decline, any promise of new jobs and a boost to the tax base are seductive, says the Reverend John H. Thomas, general minister and president of the United Church of Christ. "But communities and governmental leaders need to ask hard questions rather than simply reaching for a quick fix," he adds. "Wal-Mart does provide jobs, offer goods at reasonable prices, and pay taxes. But Wal-Mart also needs to be challenged to answer these harder questions: Does Wal-Mart really support strong, healthy families with its employment practices? Does it seek to contribute to the long-term economic health and stability of the regions where it does business? Thus far, Wal-Mart has not been able to demonstrate that it really says 'yes' to these critical questions."[3]

According to recent studies by *BusinessWeek*, *The New York Times* and *Bloomberg News*, low prices do not necessarily depend on low wages. The following are some comparisons between Wal-Mart and its archrival Costco:

- In 2005, Costco's average full-time hourly wage was $17. Wal-Mart's was $9.68.

- Costco provides much better benefits, including health care coverage, a 401(k) plan and profit-sharing. "Paying your employees well is not only the right thing to do but it makes for good business," Costco CEO James D. Sinegal told BusinessWeek.

- Only 6 percent of Costco employees leave after their first year of employment, compared to 21 percent at Sam's Club (Wal-Mart's comparable warehouse division).

- Costco's part-time workers are eligible for health insurance after six months on the job, compared with two years at Wal-Mart.

- Eighty-five percent of Costco's workers have health insurance, compared with less than half at Wal-Mart.

- Twenty percent of Costco's employees are unionized, while Wal-Mart fiercely resists unionization. "[Costco takes] a very pro-employee attitude," Rome Aloise of the Teamsters told BusinessWeek.

- In 2004, Costco's CEO James D. Sinegal earned $2.7 million in total pay; Wal-Mart's CEO, H. Lee Scott, made $17.9 million.

- From August 2004 to July 2005, Costco's stock price rose more than 10 percent, while Wal-Mart's slipped 5 percent.

- Costco is the fourth largest U.S. retailer. Wal-Mart is the world's largest corporation of any kind.

Sources: *BusinessWeek* (April 12, 2004), *The New York Times* (July 18, 2005), *Bloomberg News* (August 24, 2005)[4]

J. Bennett Guess, editor of the *United Church News,* notes that it is precisely the "Wal-Martization" of our U.S. economic system—substandard jobs, inadequate health insurance, nonexistent retirement benefits, discriminatory hiring and wage practices, and antifamily work policies—that has sustained and widened the gap between rich and poor, which we Christians profess to despise. Capitalists, like Sam Walton, should be well compensated for their ingenuity and efficiency at meeting the demands of the market. But should the billions in profit reaped by American corporate giants be dispersed only among the owners and corporate executives at the top echelons of the company? Or do those owners and executives have a moral obligation to provide livable wages and comprehensive benefits to the rank-in-file workers, whose cheap labor at the bottom sustains the millionaires at the top? The Wal-Mart scenario bespeaks a struggle that is endemic to all of corporate America. It is the struggle of how to balance profitability with moral and social responsibility. Discernment in business is required to determine when a corporation's quest for profit is promoted at the expense of people. Spiritually discerning American consumers will have to ask not only, "What is financially affordable?" We will also have to ask, "What is morally responsible?" Businesses that would be both profitable and good must covet and cultivate hearts of discernment.

DISCERNMENT IN GOVERNMENT

Persons in positions of governmental leadership and authority are entrusted with the responsibility to work for the socioeconomic well-being of the populace. Where there is a disconnect between the public and the public policies of elected officials, the morale of the country suffers and sociopolitical dissent begins to take hold.

In the ethnicity and socioeconomic status of the people who were left behind in New Orleans after the ravages of Hurricane Katrina, and in the ethnicity and socioeconomic status of the young people who rioted in Paris, France in November of 2005, God has reminded the world again that poverty and disenfranchisement still run along the fault lines of the world's racial divide. Greater discernment in public policy is required in order to understand that at the heart of much of our national and global turmoil, there is still the sin of racism and racism's pernicious legacy. Failure to accurately perceive and address this fundamental malady in our national and in our global network will continue to result in failed policies that only placate but never really resolve the iniquities and inequities of biased systems.

Political savvy, legal expertise, and degrees in public policy will not take the place of a genuine heart to serve all the people. When all of the people are not served, none of the people can ever really be at ease. Leaders must be able to make the fine distinction between that which is expedient and that which is ethical. Leaders must be able to mitigate the intricate differences and disputes among the citizens, while seeking to protect the rights of each individual. Leaders must be able to hold the delicate balances of the profitable and the prophetic in place so that our prophets are not destroyed for the sake of profits.

Private enterprise, which has the focus of making money, should never be expected to take on the mantle of governmental authority, which has the focus of serving people. Unregulated capitalism is dangerously exclusionary because it neglects those persons who have historically and systemically been denied access to capital. Indeed, capitalism works well for those who have capital. But the millions of people who struggle daily against systems of entrenched discrimination must find in their government a voice and a means to break through the "good ole boy" networks of closed capitalism. Capitalism itself must be monitored and regulated by independent governmental authorities who must work for the good of the whole society, including the disenfranchised. What's good for corporate America is not necessarily what's good for all of America. Only governmental officials with hearts of discernment can make the fine distinctions which are necessary to arbitrate the intricate discrepancies that invariably emerge between the private and the public interests of the body politic.

When offered a blank check endorsed by heaven, Solomon had the wisdom to pray for an understanding heart—a heart of discernment—so that he would be able to wisely serve the people.

THE DIVINE RESPONSE TO A WISE REQUEST

Of all the requests that Solomon could have made, God was pleased that Solomon chose to make a request that would enable him to become a better servant. Solomon did not request an increase in material, but an increase in maturity. Solomon did not ask God to give him something great; he asked God to make him a great servant. Solomon understood that his success as a leader was not dependent upon material resources nor popular opinion, but upon his ability to reflect the heart of God in every facet of his leadership and administration. God was pleased with Solomon's request. God said to Solomon:

> Since you have asked for this and not for long life or wealth for yourself, nor have asked for the death of your enemies but for discernment in administering justice, I will do what you have asked. I will give you a wise and discerning heart, so that there will never have been anyone like you, nor will there ever be. Moreover, I will give you what you have not asked for—both riches and honor—so that in your lifetime you will have no equal among kings (1 Kgs 3:11–13 NIV).

Leaders who focus upon their own self-development and self-enlightenment do themselves and the people they lead an invaluable service. What we learn from Solomon's experience is that God adds astounding bonuses to the leader who seeks to serve people with insight and integrity. Solomon's willingness to serve was enhanced with spiritual discernment, material riches, and exceptional social honor. Many leaders and the people they serve suffer for the leaders' lack of attention to his or her own growth and development.

Solomon's model of leadership is exemplary because it was born out of Solomon's desire to improve himself and to broaden his own understanding of authority. Great leadership is not something we are born into, and it is not something that is concomitant with a title, a position, an appointment, or even a majority vote. Great leadership is something we must attain prayerfully and purposefully by looking beyond the superficial and seeking God for hearts of discernment.

QUESTIONS FOR REFLECTION

1. Solomon's wisdom is often only discussed in light of what Solomon requested and received from God at Gibeon. What wisdom did Solomon evidence to God before God granted his request at Gibeon?

2. What does it mean to say that most of us can handle struggle and scarcity much better than we can handle success and abundance? Give some historical and some personal illustrations of this observation.

3. What is the significance of being grateful for what we have before we petition God for what we want?

4. How does Solomon's perception of his father David in 1 Kings 3:6 compare to your perception of your parents?

5. Think of some major transitions in your life and list the opportunities for your self-development that accompanied those transitions. Did you seize or neglect those opportunities?

6. What are some of the mistakes that have been made when persons confuse their positions of leadership with their capacity to lead? How might these mistakes have been avoided?

7. What price do we pay when we fail to admit our inadequacies as leaders?

8. How do we recognize and call forth greatness in our family members, church members, and associates? What does this say about our own self-esteem?

9. Discuss the value of a discerning heart in your personal and professional affairs.

10. What motivated Solomon's request to God at Gibeon? What particular issues arise when leaders fail to focus on their own self-development?

2

THE SECOND KEY: WORK

1 Kings 5:1–18 (The Living Bible)

1   King Hiram of Tyre had always been a great admirer of David, so when he learned that David's son Solomon was the new king of Israel, he sent ambassadors to extend congratulations and good wishes.

2, 3   Solomon replied with a proposal about the Temple of God he wanted to build. His father, David, Solomon pointed out to Hiram, had not been able to build it because of the numerous wars going on, and he had been waiting for God to give him peace.

4   "But now," Solomon said to Hiram, "my Sovereign God has given Israel peace on every side: I have no foreign enemies or internal rebellions.

5   So I am planning to build a Temple for my Sovereign God, just as God instructed my father that I should do. For God told him, 'Your son, whom I will place upon your throne, shall build me a temple.'

6   Now please assist me with this project. Send your woodsmen to the mountains of Lebanon to cut cedar timber for me, and I will send my men to work beside them, and I will pay your men whatever wages you ask: for as you know, no one in Israel can cut timber like you Sidonians!"

7   Hiram was very pleased with the message from Solomon. "Praise God for giving David a wise son to be king of the great nation of Israel," he said.

8   Then he sent his reply to Solomon: "I have received your message and I will do as you have asked concerning the timber. I can supply both cedar and cypress.

9   My men will bring the logs from the Lebanon mountains to the Mediterranean Sea and build them into rafts. We will float them along the coast to wherever you need them; then we will break the rafts apart and deliver the timber to you. You can pay me with food for my household."

10 So Hiram produced for Solomon as much cedar and cypress timber as he desired.

11 In return Solomon sent him an annual payment of 125,000 bushels of wheat for his household and 96 gallons of pure olive oil.

12 So God gave great wisdom to Solomon just as God had promised. And Hiram and Solomon made a formal alliance of peace.

13 Then Solomon drafted thirty thousand laborers from all over Israel,

14 and rotated them to Lebanon, ten thousand a month, so that each man was a month in Lebanon and two months at home. Adoniram was the general superintendent of this labor camp.

15 Solomon also had seventy thousand additional laborers, eighty thousand stone cutters in the hill country,

16 and thirty three hundred foremen.

17 The stone cutters quarried and shaped huge blocks of stone —a very expensive job—for the foundation of the Temple.

18 Men from Gebal helped Solomon's and Hiram's builders in cutting the timber and making the boards, and in preparing the stone for the Temple.

THE WORK OF DOMESTIC DEVELOPMENT

The second key to Solomon's astounding success as a leader is work. Upon Solomon's anointment and ascension to the throne of Israel, Hiram, King of Tyre (a small island located on the east coast of the Mediterranean Sea, just north of ancient Palestine) sent envoys to the young King Solomon with salutations and congratulations. Solomon used the greetings of King Hiram as an opportunity to share his vision to build a temple—a house of worship—to the glory of God.

King David, Solomon's father and predecessor, wanted to build a temple to glorify God. According to Solomon, however, his father could not because he was preoccupied with foreign wars. In this situation, we must not miss the parallel between a nation's domestic development and a nation's foreign diplomacy. King David's failure or inability to secure diplomatic peace with other nations meant that he lacked the resources of time, talent, and treasure necessary to build a temple for the glorification of God and for the edification of his people.

This is why anyone who is concerned about quality public education, adequate and affordable health care, a healthy environment, efficient transportation systems, and viable economic development in his/her immediate vicinity, must also be concerned about national foreign policy and the cost of war. The more human lives, financial resources, and national energy that we devote to foreign wars, the less able we are to engage and defeat the domestic enemies of poverty, pollution, illiteracy, and lack of opportunity.

War siphons away our national resources from the development of our own infrastructure. Military crusades detract from our ability to make adequate and substantive investments in the quality of life in our own communities. The point here is not to advocate a retreat back to the draconian notions of American isolationism. It is clear that God has placed America in a unique position of global responsibility.

Dr. William Sloane Coffin, however, in his book, *The Heart Is a Little to the Left,* makes the point that "The United States doesn't have to lead the world; it has to first join it. Then, with greater humility, it can play a wiser leadership role."[1]

The leadership responsibility that America has in the world today is not that of advancing American unilateralism or Western cultural and economic hegemony. Our responsibility is to take the leadership in building dialogue and diplomacy with the international community. By doing this, we can foster peaceful coexistence and respect for diversity around the planet.

The prerequisite to international peace has always been international justice. A compelling case can be made that the ranks of the Nazis were and the ranks of terrorists are filled with persons who for years have been seething with resentment. They are angered over issues that they presume the superpowers have neglected or failed to adequately address. According to Bishop Desmond Tutu of South Africa, the war against terrorism will never be won as long as situations that make people desperate are allowed to exist.[2]

While this argument does not intend to excuse the violent attack of unsuspecting civilians, when we fail to address the pressing issues of international injustice, we only help to create desperate individuals who become prime prospects for induction into the ranks of violent extremists. Former U.S. President Jimmy Carter has warned America on more than one occasion about the connections between American policy toward the Palestinians and the attacks of September 11, 2001.

It is America's long-standing perceived bias in favor of Israel that has contributed significantly toward the anti-American sentiment evidenced throughout much of the Muslim world. Would not a committment to help judiciously negotiate the disputes between Israel and Palestine have been diplomatically far wiser for our nation than reacting to the pent-up anti-American vitriol that exploded upon us on September 11? A preemptive attack on injustice is much wiser, much more efficient, and much more effective than a preemptive military attack on a declared enemy.

During the years of our contentious war in Vietnam, Dr. Martin Luther King Jr. spoke to the nation's conscience. He warned us that we could not, at the same time, effectively wage a war on poverty at home and a war in Vietnam overseas. Dr. King tried to tell America that the bombs we dropped in Vietnam would explode in our own backyards. The explosion would be rampant violence on our city streets, increased unemployment, rising poverty levels, and pervasive social unrest, and the dilution of our democratic infrastructures.

Dr. King's prophecy has proven to be correct. Since we have set ourselves on a course of national hegemony instead of international diplomacy, and since we have opted to invest in military might instead of the United Nations, our national surpluses have been turned into national deficits. In addition, while social programs to aid the poor and the disenfranchised have been severely slashed, the barometers of dissent and discord in our country have risen to record levels. Our bellicose rhetoric, our unilateral resolve, and our determined pursuit of a vengeful war have left us drained and deterred from the full pursuit of our own domestic revitalization.

Like King David, we cannot fully engage in foreign wars and fully advance our domestic development simultaneously. King David could not build a temple in Jerusalem because he was too busy fueling, financing, and advancing military exploits. And, he could not adequately invest in peace and prosperity within Israel until peace and prosperity could be established outside of Israel.

THE WORK TO ADD VALUE TO YOUR ASSIGNMENT

Once Israel was able to establish peace with its neighbors, the stage was set for the enhancement of its own culture. With peace at every border and with no foreign enemies or internal rebellions, Solomon prepared to build a temple in Jerusalem to the glory of God. We should note that Solomon could have rested and been content to recline in the lavish comfort of his royal inheritance.

Solomon was already wealthy; he had already ascended to the throne of Israel and found favor among the people; he already possessed exceptional wisdom and wealth. To coin a contemporary colloquialism, he was already *phat!* But notwithstanding, all of the substantial assets of his inheritance, Solomon still purposed to take upon himself the work of building a temple to the glory of God and for the edification of his people. In his willingness to do so, Solomon purposed to add value to his assignment as well as to the life of his nation.

"Added value" is a precious attribute of any worker in any organization. In fact, it is what separates an exceptional worker from an average worker. Average workers only do enough to get by and draw a paycheck. Exceptional workers, on the other hand, bring creativity, enthusiasm, and resourcefulness to their assignments. Instead of complaining about the way things are, exceptional workers take the initiative to make things better. Instead of seeking to avoid responsibility, exceptional workers take on the responsibility to help improve the culture and the quality controls of their organization. Instead of maintaining a job, exceptional workers add value to their work assignments.

Solomon could have easily rested upon the laurels of his famous father and simply maintained that which had already been established and bequeathed to him. But instead, without coercion or constraint, Solomon purposed within himself to add value to his assignment and his realm by building upon that which he had been given.

It's one thing to maintain an inheritance; it's another thing to build upon it. It's one thing to occupy a position; it's another thing to fill the position with so much creativity and commitment that the person in the position becomes vital to the well-being of the entire organization. In the life of an organization, positions are constantly being reviewed, altered, and sometimes phased out. But persons who add value to their positions by distinguishing themselves through hard work, reliability, and resourcefulness have been known to grow their positions and, in some cases, even to create new positions. Even as positions phase out, new positions are identified and created all the time for valuable workers who add value to their work assignments. Even in times of fiscal cutbacks and downsizing, there is always an attempt made to retain those valued employees who add value to their assignments as well as the overall culture of the organization. Valuable employees grow positions and help to create new positions by going above and beyond their job description to enhance their professional performance and cultural climate of their organizations.

It is especially incumbent upon those of us who work in ministry to "add value" to our work assignments. In the lesson on stewardship given by Jesus in the twenty-fifth chapter of Matthew's Gospel, the steward who received one "talent" was judged by his lord not for failing to maintain, but for failing to add value to that which he'd been given. His one talent was taken from him because he failed to add anything to it. God certainly intends for all of us in ministry to grow our ministries, and yet we should never forget that in the realm of God, growth is not necessarily measured numerically, but spiritually and in terms of maturity. Growing out is not tantamount to growing up.

THE VALUE OF A SOLID WORK ETHIC

The erection of the Temple in Jerusalem for the glorification of God and for edification of God's people was a mammoth undertaking. It could not have been accomplished without a deeply concerted effort and tremendous amount of hard work. Solomon was willing to accept the challenge. He was willing to devote the energy, effort, resources, and time it would require to bring his divine vision into human reality. In essence, Solomon was willing to go to work.

For many people, the one thing that separates their visions from reality is their work ethic. Great visions require great commitments to labor. In fact, the greater the vision, the greater will be the demand on time, energy, and resources. Nehemiah 4:6 tells us, "So we rebuilt the wall . . . for the people had a mind to work." Like the building of the Temple, the rebuilding of the walls of Jerusalem required a strong work ethic.

The truth is that every worker does not possess "a mind to work." Sometimes we have a mind to "get over" and to "get by" while doing as little as possible. Sometimes we have a mind to dodge responsibility and pass our work on to others. The work of reigning in our national deficit and bringing our deficit spending to an end will require some hard work on behalf of our elected officials and on behalf of the overall American citizenry. But instead of taking the bull by the horns and doing the hard work that is needed to cut the pork, eliminate wasteful spending, monitor our efficiency, and prioritize our spending, we allow our elected officials to perpetuate the deficit cycles of tax and spend (Democrats) or tax rebate to the wealthy and spend (Republicans).

The work that we fail to do in reigning in our deficit spending today will saddle future generations with higher interest rates and a devalued dollar. Hard work may require great sacrifices from each of us today, but work that is avoided and perpetually postponed will cost us even more in the future.

THE WORK TO BUILD BROAD-BASED COALITIONS
The work of God's realm is too broad, too expansive, and too encompassing to be accomplished within the parochial

perimeters of tribalism. What God calls us to do is much greater than what can be accomplished by ourselves or our clan. The work of God's realm always requires us to reach beyond ourselves and our cultural context. The work of God's realm will always require us to reach beyond ourselves and our cultural context. The work of God's realm requires us to build working partnerships with others and to establish broad-based coalitions of consensus. These broad-based coalitions must often be established with persons who are outside of our race, class, culture, and religion. Solomon's work for the realm was so broad and so expansive that it required the involvement and investment of people who were outside of Solomon's culture, ethnicity, and faith tradition. In his work to erect a temple dedicated to the worship of the Most High God, Solomon found it necessary to enlist the support of King Hiram and the Sidonians or Canaanites. In so doing, Solomon had to step outside the conventions of his culture.

The Canaanites were routinely looked down upon and regarded as dogs by the then prevailing religious orthodoxy of his Jewish culture. But the work of God's realm is much bigger and much broader than the dictums of any one religious tradition or the catechisms of any one cultural convention. In a time of rampant ethnocentrism, reinforced by religion, among a people who prided themselves on their claims of religious and cultural superiority, Solomon understood that the work of God's realm could not be limited to his own nation, his own culture, or his own faith tradition. The work of God's realm always requires us to reach beyond ourselves and our contexts of comfortable familiarity.

The Israelites were and still are a gifted and an anointed people. But in order to build God's Temple, they needed wood that they did not possess and they needed skilled woodcutters whom they could not provide from among their own ranks. For the sake of the realm, they had to reach out and build broad-based coalitions with other people. Solomon would never have been able to get the job done had he been so fixated upon his own national religious pride that he could not reach beyond the borders of his own people and establish collaborative coalitions with people from other cultures, other races, and other religious perspectives. Too often the work of God's realm is stunted and stymied by believers who are oblivious to the value of diversity due to the conceit of their religious arrogance.

At a time when the work of building a global community requires the enlistment of all faith traditions and cultural perspectives, many people of faith are actually retreating back into the rigid enclaves of religious fundamentalism. The absolute moral claims of religious fundamentalists, which are intolerant of other religious expressions and incapable of embracing cultural diversity, are dangerous and detrimental to the work of peace and coexistence in the world. Whether it takes the form of the Taliban in Afghanistan or the ultraconservatives in Israel or the Shiite radicals in Iraq or the Christian Right in America, religious fundamentalism is dangerous because its exclusive truth claims leave no room for the establishment of broad-based partnerships and expansive ecumenical collaboration. The growing tide of religious intolerance is precisely what is fueling the national and international culture wars of our day and consequently impeding the work toward world peace.

The work of God's realm is big enough and broad enough to employ the services of "whosoever will." Even persons who may not believe in God the way we believe in God and reverence the Bible the way we reverence the Bible can still respect our work if it is performed with the intent to include rather than exclude. In my ministry at the Victory Church of Stone Mountain, Georgia, I strive earnestly to keep our doors and our ministries open to "whosoever will." Everyone in our community does not belong to our church, but our church belongs to everyone in our community—regardless of race, gender, culture, class, or sexual orientation.

In my nineteen years as pastor and organizer of the Victory Church, it has been my privilege to say to Jews, Muslims, Buddhists, agnostics, seekers, conservatives, progressives, and religious and nonreligious individuals: "No matter who you are, or where you are on life's journey, you are welcome here." I have discovered that the work to uplift and empower our community is too broad to be confined to our congregational catechisms. Victory is therefore, always looking for opportunities to reach beyond itself to partner with other people of good will who share our interest in community development.

Such a perspective, in my estimation, is not antithetical to the Christian gospel. I believe that Jesus Christ is the eternal personification and embodiment of universal love, and I believe that Jesus was crucified at Calvary precisely because he refused to limit God's love to any one class, nation, or religious persuasion. It is precisely because Jesus manifested the love of God to persons outside his religious tradition that he was killed by the traditionalists of his own religion. In his resurrection, however, Jesus demonstrated that he would not be constrained by religious convention, nor confined by cultural exclusivism. He arose from the dead as Savior, Redeemer, and Reconciler of the whole wide world. Absolutely no one lives outside the purview of Christ's grace, love, and mercy. No religion can contain him; no cultural expression can exhaust him; no nation can confine him; and no grave can keep him from advancing the all inclusive love of Almighty God for all humankind.

As a Christian, I believe that a vision of ministry that includes and transcends Christendom is the truest expression of God's love in Christ Jesus. Many of the people who benefit from the educational, recreational, financial, and empowerment ministries of Victory do not attend Victory, and some do not adhere to doctrines of Christianity. I believe that the Victory Church's ministry of service (not proselytization) to these people is in keeping with our gospel mandate. Our work must be broader than our membership; our reach must be beyond our pews; our ministries must go outside of our stained glass; our love must transcend our congregation; and our perception of God's presence must not be limited to our own religious tradition.

Serving as president of the DeKalb County (Georgia) Branch of the NAACP, I have still another vehicle for broad-based community outreach and empowerment. My work in the civil rights arena has again reminded me of the necessity of building broad-based coalitions. The campaign against racial injustice cannot be accomplished in a vacuum.

Justice is indeed indivisible—a threat to justice anywhere is a threat to justice everywhere. Oppressive systems have long since prospered via the methodology of "divide and conquer," employed to keep oppressed groups fighting one another. Oppressed people who expend their resources and energy fighting other oppressed people have little or nothing left to confront the systems that victimize all oppressed people.

During the national debates concerning gay marriage that preceded the 2004 presidential elections, the Reverend Gregory Daniels, an African American Evangelical pastor from Chicago, was quoted as saying: "If the KKK opposed gay marriage, I would ride with them." Apparently, Reverend Daniels is not aware that the Ku Klux Klan is as virulent in its hatred of blacks as it is in its hatred of homosexuals. Reverend Daniels would have only been able to ride with the KKK from the lynching of a homosexual to his own lynching. There is a direct line of venom between Eric Rudolf's bombing of an abortion clinic in Birmingham and his bombing of a lesbian night club in Atlanta. The truth is that many of today's homophobes, sexists, and anti-modernists are the ideological descendents of yesterday's racists and anti-Semites.

The future viability of civil rights organizations lies in our willingness to step outside the vacuum of our own struggle for racial justice and build dynamic partnerships with other progressive movements that are struggling to overcome injustice in various other dimensions.

Joe Klein, editorialist for *Time* magazine, opines that it is time to move beyond race-based aggrievement to something more inclusive. He notes that there are nearly twice as many poor white people living in the United States as poor blacks; the black poverty rate diminished dramatically—from 33.4 percent to 22.5 percent—during the Clinton administration, while it has risen 24.7 percent under Bush; and the recent increase in poverty has been most pronounced among Hispanics.[3]

Klein concludes that the most effective thing the Congressional Black Caucus could do to fight poverty would probably be to invite white and Hispanic legislators who have significant numbers of poor people in their districts to join its ranks and rename itself the Congressional Antipoverty Caucus. Additionally, he argues that the most effective way to build a coalition to fight poverty and preserve affirmative action in this conservative era would be to base preferences on economic needs rather than race. Solomon teaches us that there is wisdom in Klein's observations.

Truthfully, there are increasing numbers of African Americans who suffer not just because of racism, but because of caste systems of poverty, poor educational opportunities, and poor health care, as well as the classism, sexism, and heterosexism that plague significant segments of the black community.

No honest and informed individual can deny that white racism is still the enduring original sin of America. It helped to create the culture of poverty existent in places like the Ninth Ward of New Orleans. George W. Bush's dominant Republican Party was reborn in racism, having sided with Southern segregationists in the 1960s. Notwithstanding all of that, as well as the continuing need to remain vigilant in the fight against the racism of the twenty-first century, civil rights leaders and organizations must be willing to align themselves with the masses of people from all races who confront economic oppression and social disenfranchisement in myriad forms on a daily basis.

Dr. Cornell West argues that the debates regarding hierarchies of oppression—that is, "whose oppression is the greatest?"—are futile and mutually detrimental to all oppressed people. I believe that before his death Dr. Martin Luther King Jr. began, not to deny, but to transcend the race issue by moving his civil rights movement closer to becoming a human rights movement through the Poor People's Campaign. A human rights focus is, I believe, the best way to galvanize all of the disenfranchised and to affirm the rights of everyone.

Racism, sexism, homophobia, and militarism are four heads to the same monster. This multifaceted beast of systemic oppression can only be defeated as freedom movements and civil rights organizations move beyond myopic agendas and band together in broad-based solidarity to advance the common goal of "one nation, under God, indivisible, with freedom and justice for all."

Under the prophetic leadership of Dr. Martin Luther King Jr., the civil rights movement brought down the bastions of segregation and racial discrimination—not just for African Americans but for countless women, immigrants, and other minorities throughout the country. The civil rights achievements of the 1960s, which effectively changed the history and destiny of America, did not come about by an exclusive focus on racial issues alone.

Dr. King's vision of "the beloved community" was so big and so broad that it left no one behind. Like King Solomon, Dr. King was perceptive enough to reach beyond his own people and build partnerships with persons of various cultural views and religious persuasions. Under Dr. King's leadership, the civil rights movement included persons of the Jewish faith, white liberals from the north, disenfranchised people of all races, and eventually young conscientious Americans decrying their nation's involvement in the quagmire called the Vietnam War.

Dr. King's visionary, broad-based coalition serves as a model to inspire freedom movements in America and around the globe. From the valiant movement to bring down the bastions of apartheid in South Africa to the courageous stand against fascism in Tiananmen Square in Beijing, to the determined refusal to succumb to the violations of heterosexist intimidation at Stone Wall in New York City, to the explosive resistance to French ethnocentrism made by young French citizens of North African descent, freedom fighters of every cultural and religious distinction resonate with the all-inclusive mandates of Dr. King's vision of "the beloved community." If America is to continue to make progress for the betterment of all its citizens and for the peace of the global community, the impetus for the establishment of broad-based coalitions must be revived.

THE WORK TO PROVIDE OPPORTUNITIES FOR MEANINGFUL EMPLOYMENT

Coalition and collaboration with persons outside of one's group is essential to the work of God's realm. King Hiram and the Phoenecians, or the Canaanites, had their own culture, their own ethnic identity, and their own religion apart from the Jews, but when King Solomon invited them to take part in the realization of the vision God had given him, King Hiram praised God and readily agreed to work with King Solomon.

As a result of the intercultural coalition established between them, an escalation of employment throughout that region of the Middle East was brought about. The work of God's realm provides opportunity for persons not only to work and make money, but to work and find fulfillment in contributing to an endeavor that glorifies God and edifies people. The glorification of God and the edification of people are the two concomitant dimensions of the work of God's realm. It can be argued theologically that whenever people are edified, God is glorified. God would be glorified and people would be edified not only in the Temple after its construction. God would be glorified and people would be edified during the phase of the Temple's construction itself, because that phase enabled people to find meaningful employment. The work of God's realm, as facilitated through Solomon, offered persons an opportunity not just to make money, but to find meaning in life through a work related vocation.

Solomon said to Hiram, "Get your people to cut down the cedar trees in Lebanon, and I will send a cadre of my own people to work beside your people—perhaps to learn how you cut trees so well—and I will pay you whatever wages you ask." Hiram responded, "I will do as you have asked concerning the timber, and I will supply you with both cedar and cypress trees—as much as you want. Then, I'll have my men bring the logs to the Mediterranean Sea and build them into rafts. We will then float the rafts along the coast to wherever you need them. Then we'll break the rafts apart and deliver the timber to you. You can pay me with food for my household" (1 Kgs 5:6–9).

Solomon's vision to advance the work of God's realm through the erection of the Temple in Jerusalem spurred economic development throughout that region of the Middle East in ninth century B.C.E. The construction of the Temple was certainly one of the largest capital enterprises of the day. It put tens of thousands of people to work throughout the region and forged an international economic coalition between Israel and its neighbors that greatly enhanced the peace, prosperity, and stability of the region as a whole.

Solomon drafted thirty thousand laborers from all over Israel and rotated them into work forces in Lebanon. Moreover, Solomon had seventy thousand additional laborers, eighty thousand stonecutters in the hill country and thirty three hundred foremen. Workers from Gebal, another Phoenician city located near present-day Beirut, worked along with Solomon's and Hiram's builders to cut the timber, make the boards, and prepare the stone for the Temple. This was a massive work force and a major impetus for economic development—all made possible because Solomon had a vision to glorify God and to edify people through the construction of the Temple in Jerusalem. That vision put people of various cultural perspectives to work with purposeful employment.

Imagine what a different place the Middle East would be today if the focus of the region had remained upon intercultural economic collaboration and development instead of religious ideology and geographic domination. Comprehensive economic development can only flourish in a political climate that fosters a mutuality of respect and a concern for the economic viability of all persons involved. Solomon would very likely not have been successful in advancing such a major enterprise if he had attempted to limit the benefits of the project exclusively to the people of his nation.

The nationalist, terrorist, and ultraconservative forces operating in the Middle East today have crippled its economic development and brought havoc upon the entire region. The economic stability and viability of Israel is inextricably intertwined with the economic stability and viability of Palestine as well as all the other Middle Eastern countries. The work of God's realm cannot be accomplished in a vacuum of nationalistic pride or religious arrogance. The economic stability and viability of some is contingent upon the economic stability and viability of all parties concerned. Even on foreign soil, God's people are admonished to "seek the peace and prosperity of the city to which I have carried you into exile. Pray to God for it, because if it prospers, you too will prosper." (Jer. 29:7 NIV).

Facing the economic depression of the 1930s, President Franklin D. Roosevelt had some tough decisions to make. The crucial question was how to rebuild America and put Americans back to work. Roosevelt's answer to this pressing issue was the New Deal. In this initiative, FDR rejected what later came to be called "voodoo economics"—the notion that feeding corporate America would itself propel employment and economic growth in the general populace.

The New Deal initiative did not cater to the top of America's economic pyramid with the euphemistic expectation that the benefits realized at the top would trickle down to those at the bottom. Instead, the New Deal started with a concern for the widest, most essential sector of the American population—the American workers. In focusing upon the needs of the common laborer, the New Deal recruited and galvanized the vast resources of corporate America into the service of the public good. The New Deal provided employment and economic opportunities for the American worker that the basic market demands of unregulated capitalism had ignored.

The Public Works Projects of the New Deal basically rebuilt the infrastructure of America, helped to restore public confidence in the good will of government, and provided meaningful employment to countless American families who had been lost in the ravages of the Great Depression. Like Solomon's plan for the erection of the Temple in Jerusalem, FDR's New Deal brought a vision of God's realm into line with the economic needs of society. As a result, persons in Israel under Solomon and persons in America under FDR found opportunity not just to make money, but to contribute to the noble goal of glorifying God through edifying and empowering people.

FDR was elected to an unprecedented fourth term in 1944. By then it was apparent that Nazi Germany would be defeated, and Allied leaders began to plan the post–World War II future. FDR proposed the United Nations for the peaceful balance of power in the global community. As the successor to the League of Nations, the United Nations was designed to foster a global forum of international interchange that would connect every nation of the world into a network of diplomacy. This international network would hopefully diminish the prospects of further worldwide confrontations. Like Solomon, FDR understood that international diplomacy would be infinitely less costly and infinitely more beneficial than international war.

Although President Franklin Roosevelt died just before World War II ended, under his leadership, America invested considerable energies and resources to the establishment of the United Nations. The UN was, in effect, FDR's response to the debacle and destruction of World War II. Despite the fact that the UN is by no means a perfect organization (it has no enforcement capacities outside of the volunteer regiments of its member nations and its ability to convince the superpowers), it has given a global voice to scores of small nations. These nations might otherwise be completely ignored, and it has helped to call worldwide attention and relief to countless disasters and trouble spots around the globe.

Notwithstanding its many imperfections, the absence of the United Nations would leave the nations of the world even more disconnected and separated than they are today. In a historical context of rigid ethnocentrism, Solomon connected the resources of his people to the resources of other nations and cultures. In so doing, Solomon actually set a new precedent for international diplomacy and global unity. Solomon and FDR both understood that the economic advancement of their nations could not be accomplished unilaterally. In America, the resurgent economy after World War II was possible in part because international peace was established. And in Israel, a Temple to the glory of God could only be erected while international coalitions were fostered.

Today in America, the signature initiatives of the FDR administration are under attack and in grave danger of being effectively dismantled. Today, more than a few persons in pivotal positions of authority reject the notion that the primary responsibility of government is to protect and provide for the public good—even if it means the regulation of private enterprise and the incentivization of corporate investment into the public sector.

Today, our nation's priorities have shifted from a concern for the common worker to a bold bolstering of the military-industrial complex, coupled with an unashamed acquiescence to the interest of the corporate elite. Abortion, gay marriage, school vouchers, stem cell research, and the public display of the Ten Commandments are mere smokescreens designed to distract the nation's attention from the basic attack on the economic philosophy of the New Deal as well as the attempted reversal of the socioeconomic gains for minorities made as a result of civil rights struggles of the 1960s.

The attempt to dismantle Social Security instead of a concerted effort to save Medicare/Medicaid is but one example of the effort to do away with the social programs that have fostered the social advancement of poor and working-class Americans for the past sixty years. Consequently, poor and working-class Americans of all races, genders, cultures, and sexual orientations stand to lose the most as the nation retreats from the vision of public works into a cocoon of unregulated capitalism sanctioned by Christian evangelical right wing conservatives.

The real issue for leaders today is whether or not true socioeconomic progress can be made without a focus on the common laborer domestically, and international diplomacy, globally. With more and more of American real estate in the hands of foreign investors and the likelihood of increased out-sourcing of American jobs in the coming years, the prospects of the American worker are no longer exclusively in the hands of Americans.

Solomon illustrates for us how a concern for the common laborer coupled with a concern for foreign relations can escalate employment both at home and abroad. Because Solomon decided to build the Temple to the glory of God in Jerusalem, people found work and families were fed throughout the coasts of the eastern Mediterranean. In return for the cedar and cypress woods he supplied, King Hiram said to Solomon, "You can pay me with food for my people" (1 Kings 5:9). Solomon said "yes" to God's work in Jerusalem, and as a result people had bread to eat in Tyre, Lebanon, and Gebal.

When leaders say "yes" to work that glorifies God and edifies people (realm work) they bless the lives of countless others by providing opportunity for meaningful employment. In 1959, Berry Gordy borrowed eight hundred dollars from his family members to start his own record label in Detroit, called Tamla. The same year, he incorporated a second record label and called it Motown, in honor of the "Motor City"—Detroit. Motown soon grew into the largest independent record company in Detroit, providing employment to hundreds of singers, dancers, songwriters, musicians, and technicians who otherwise might have found little or no outlet to utilize their God-given talents. Motown provided a viable avenue through which the music of the soul embedded in the black church could be brought onto the national and international stage as soul music, or rhythm and blues.

Although the music of Motown was not expressly religious in lyric, no one can deny that it emanated directly from the passion, energy, and ethos of the black church. The same spiritual energy that inspired the spirituals inspired the blues, and the same spiritual energy that inspires sacred music in the black church inspires soul music in the broader American context. To the extent that Motown was able to weave the musical genius of the black church into the cultural fabric of America, God was glorified and people were edified.

Motown was more than a means to just make money. Motown was a vehicle that enhanced and enlivened the culture of America with divine inspiration straight from the black church. What would American music be today without the rich contributions of Smokey Robinson, Mary Wells, the Temptations, Marvin Gaye, Diana Ross and the Supremes, Martha and the Vandellas, the Four Tops, Stevie Wonder, Gladys Knight and the Pips, the Isley Brothers, the Jackson Five, and the Funk Brothers? Think of how many studio technicians, cosmetologists, choreographers, stage managers, business managers, concert promoters, bus drivers, costume designers, disc jockeys, and wig manufacturers would have been denied meaningful employment if Berry Gordy had not worked to advance a vision of the realm that glorified God by edifying people. A leader's vision carries the potential of blessing the lives of countless others with meaningful employment and purposeful careers.

THE WORK TO FOSTER COMMUNITY DEVELOPMENT

To be sure, churches throughout the various communities of our nation have done even more to inspire people, feed families, and call persons out of indifferent idleness into significant service than Motown. As churches continue to embrace a vision of community empowerment, they serve as vital engines for the economic advancement of their communities. Job training, job fairs, computer labs, media suites, bookstores, libraries, business development workshops, education in budgeting and investing, home-buying seminars, scholarship funds, investment clubs, and church academies are but a few of the ways churches contribute to the economic viability of their communities.

Along with a solid theological education, persons with degrees in business administration, marketing, and information technology are vital to the realm work of the church and the economic viability of the communities they serve.

Through the ministry of Zion Baptist Church in Philadel -
phia, the Reverend Leon Sullivan launched a mission to create
more jobs for the people of his community. He organized pas-
tors from more than four hundred black congregations and
implemented a strategy called "selective patronage," meaning, "Don't buy where you don't work." It was through these
boycotts that businesses were forced to hire more minorities.

Reverend Sullivan discovered, however, that many minorities were unprepared for jobs. This led him to establish
the Opportunities Industrialization Centers (OIC), which
provided basic job-training skills for many unskilled minorities seeking employment. There are over seventy OIC centers
across the nation, and thirty-three centers in eighteen different countries. In 1975, Reverend Sullivan was described as
"the most hated man in South Africa" due to his efforts to
end apartheid in that country.

In 1977 he developed the "Sullivan Principles," a code of
conduct for human rights and equal opportunity for compa-
nies operating in South Africa. The Sullivan Principles are acknowledged to have been one of the most effective efforts to
end discrimination against blacks in the workplace in South
Africa and to have contributed significantly to the dismantling
of apartheid. To further expand human rights and economic
development in all communities, Reverend Sullivan created
the Global Sullivan Principles of Social Responsibility in
1997.[4] Inasmuch as Leon Sullivan has used his calling as a servant of God to foster economic development for his community, and for countless other communities beyond his own, he
has kept the spirit and the legacy of King Solomon alive.

While religious organizations can play a significant role in
helping to foster the economic empowerment of a community, religious organizations should not be expected to take
the place of the government in providing a safety net for the
millions of people who are locked into cycles of poverty. The
funds offered by the government in the Bush administra-

tion's faith-based initiative are not commensurate with the funds that have been cut from governmental social programs in order to provide tax breaks to the wealthy, economic subsidies to megacorporations, and pork barrel funding at the disposal of politicians in power.

Faith-based funding is not an adequate replacement for the governmental funding of vital social programs designed to assist those who historically and systematically have been disenfranchised. Additionally, the intermingling of church funds and government funds, which the faith-based initiative allows, jeopardizes the separation of church and state.

Independent community development corporations (CDCs) affiliated with religious organizations are the best vehicles to ensure that tax dollars are not being spent to subsidize any particular faith tradition. Independent CDCs can also ensure that the protections against discrimination based on race, religion, gender, and sexual orientation are adhered to when tax dollars are dispersed.

Finally, while religious organizations can partner with governmental agencies to provide community services, religious organizations must remain independent enough of governmental influence to serve as the conscience of the government, not just the cosigner of the government. Moses would never have been able to lead the children of Israel out of Egyptian bondage if his movement depended on subsidies from the Egyptian Pharaoh. Religious organizations must maintain a certain independence from the government to speak truth to power. And government must maintain a certain independence from religious organizations to serve all religious and nonreligious citizens fairly without bias toward any particular religious conviction—or lack thereof.

Solomon's work of building the Temple in Jerusalem provides for us a model of economic enterprise at its best. Through this work of the realm, international coalitions were established, natural resources were developed, thousands of people found employment, and the masses discovered purpose and pride in their labor. The work of God's realm is essential to the development of human community. Consequently, the work of the ministry should never be viewed as tangential to the work of community development. The work of the realm provides the venue through which our spiritual and commercial interests are reconciled to the purposes of glorifying God through edifying people. The work of God's realm brings our occupations into sync with our vocations.

This is why no leader should settle for mediocrity or incompetence in advancing the work of God's realm, even if that mediocrity or incompetence emanates from a faithful church member. Too many lives and destinies are riding on the work of the realm, and it must never be held hostage to the caprice of personal and sentimental affections. If Solomon's goal was to reward his own clan, he could have attempted to make the erection of the Temple an "in house" project, benefiting Israel alone. Solomon, however, wanted to build a temple to glorify God. This meant that he had to step outside his circle and recruit the best people available, regardless of his personal affections and affiliations. The work of God's realm must not be designated according to nepotism or seniority. Leaders must ensure that the work of God's realm is engaged with the utmost competence, commitment, and accountability. Anything less would be a disservice to people and an insult to God.

QUESTIONS FOR REFLECTION

1. How does a nation's foreign policy relate to its domestic development?

2. How do you currently "add value" to your work assignment and your work environment?

3. How does a solid work environment impact our future costs?

4. How does failure to build broad-based coalitions hamper the work of God? How effective have broad-based coalitions been in promoting the prosperity of your community?

5. What is the difference between an occupation and a vocation? Why should the two not be separated?

6. How has the "Wal-Martization" of America impacted your community and your employment?

7. How does global stability impact your local economy?

8. What dangers emerge when the faith-based initiative is allowed to replace governmental funding for social services?

9. In doing God's work, what are the dangers of nepotism?

3

THE THIRD KEY: WORSHIP

1 Kings 8:1–11

1 Then Solomon assembled the elders of Israel and all the heads of the tribes, the leaders of the ancestral houses of the Israelites, before King Solomon in Jerusalem, to bring up the ark of the covenant of God out of the city of David, which is Zion.

2 All the people of Israel assembled to King Solomon at the festival in the month Ethanim, which is the seventh month.

3 And all the elders of Israel came, and the priests carried the ark.

4 So they brought up the ark of God, the tent of meeting, and all the holy vessels that were in the tent; the priests and the Levites brought them up.

5 King Solomon and all the congregation of Israel, who had assembled before him, were with him before the ark, sacrificing so many sheep and oxen that they could not be counted or numbered.

6 Then the priests brought the ark of the covenant of God to its place, in the inner sanctuary of the house, in the most holy place, underneath the wings of the cherubim.

7 For the cherubim spread out their wings over the place of the ark, so that the cherubim made a covering above the ark and its poles.

8 The poles were so long that the ends of the poles were seen from the holy place in front of the inner sanctuary; but they could not be seen from outside; they are there to this day.

9 There was nothing in the ark except the two tables of stone that Moses had placed there at Horeb, where the Lord made a covenant with the Israelites, when they came out of the land of Egypt.

10 And when the priests came out of the holy place, a cloud filled the house of God,

11 So that the priests could not stand to minister because of the cloud; for the glory of God filled the house of God.

According to 1 Kings 6:37, it took seven years for Solomon and his collaborative consortium of economic developers and workers to build the Temple in Jerusalem to glorify God. The Temple was built with the most skilled laborers and the finest of materials: exquisite cedar and cypress wood from Lebanon, precious stone from the Palestinian hill country, ornately designed hand carvings and pure gold, which overlaid the altar and inner sanctuary of the Temple. The Temple's erection spurred economic development throughout the region of the Middle East—particularly along the eastern coast of the Mediterranean.

When this seven-year enterprise of international collaboration, human resource development, and economic stimulation was completed, King Solomon summoned and assembled the elders and leaders from every tribe of Israel together at Jerusalem for the purpose of dedicating the Temple. The dedication of the Temple was a festival of worship, which lasted for seven days. It was a time for the nation's spirit to be revived through sacred assembly, solemn reflection, grateful offerings of sacrifice, and intercessory prayer, which petitioned God for mercy upon the nation. In his wisdom,

Solomon decided that seven years of the nation's work should culminate in a national convocation of dedicatory worship. The third key to Solomon's success is worship.

WORSHIP CALLS OUR WORK TO A STANDARD OF EXCELLENCE

For people of faith, the aims of our labor are all culminated in worship. Worship is that which gives our work its meaning and purpose. Worship is that which unites our temporal occupations with our spiritual vocations. Worship is that which lifts our labor out of the mundane and places it within the providence of God's blessed will. It is only when our work finds its purpose and its culmination in our worship that we are then assured that our labors are not in vain.

So many people spend the majority of their days toiling in occupations that for them have no significance beyond a means to pay bills. Is there any wonder why there is so much despondency, frustration, and depression in the workplace? It is because so much of our job performance has no connection to our devotion to God. When our daily occupation has no connection with our spiritual devotion, we simply bide the time, do the minimum, watch the clock, and dread having to do it all again on the next work day.

When we perform without purpose and work without worship, we are consumed with a foreboding sense that our work is in vain. We may work well, we may work hard, and we may work long, but if we give our time and energy on a daily basis to that which does not reflect our calling and our purpose in God; if there is no purpose beyond a paycheck; if our labor has no everlasting consequence and no divine design, then our work is in vain. When our work becomes an expression of our worship, then whatever we do, we do it to the glory of God (1 Cor. 10:31).

If we enter data into a computer, we should do it accurately, so that God is glorified with every entry. If we answer the telephone, we should attempt to be as courteous and as helpful as possible, remembering that Jesus is on the main line, listening to every conversation. If we teach students, we should aim to offer ourselves as the best illustrations of educational enlightenment that is grounded in an abiding trust in God. If we work in finance, we should strive for the utmost accuracy and accountability, understanding the many dangers that accompany the love of money. If we work in law enforcement we should earnestly endeavor not to be cocky, never forgetting that "unless God watches over the city, the watchmen stand guard in vain" (Ps. 127:1 NIV).

If we take orders in a drive-through, we should not forget that we are not simply serving nameless customers; we are serving those who have been created in God's image. If we work in government, we should seek justice and equality for all, never forgetting that a nation's strength is not reflected in how it caters to the high and mighty, but in how it attends to the needs of "the least of these."

On one occasion, Dr. Martin Luther King Jr. said:

> If you are a street sweeper, sweep streets like Michaelangelo painted portraits; sweep streets like Beethoven composed symphonies; sweep streets like Paul Laurence Dunbar wrote poetry; like Marion Anderson sang opera, and like Harriett Tubman led the underground railroad. Sweep streets until the hosts of all time and eternity pause and say: "There goes a great street sweeper who swept his [her] job well."[1]

When our work becomes an expression of our worship, we work with excellence as our aim. Indeed, our work performance is enhanced and inspired by our spiritual purpose.

WORSHIP PROVIDES THE RENEWAL NEEDED TO STAY PRODUCTIVE

Work without worship is not only futile, it can also be exhausting. After seven years of laboring to build the temple, Solomon called the people of Israel together for a national observance of dedicatory worship. In so doing, Solomon provided opportunity for the spirit of the people to be renewed. People who are so busy working that they have no time for worship are often fatigued, irritable, cantankerous, and on the verge of mental and/or spiritual collapse. Worship provides us with more than rest; it provides us with restoration. People often neglect worship in their constant quest for more rest. But even after ten to twelve hours of sleep, we can wake up rested in body but still troubled in mind.

We can relax at home and still not be revived in spirit. We can plan exciting excursions for recreation and still not be re-created in our souls. We can go on a vacation and return with a vexation. We can go to "happy hour," stay for five hours, and then leave happy hour unhappy. A genuine renewal of heart, mind, body, and soul requires much more than rest and relaxation. It requires spiritual regeneration, mental renewal, and soul revival. This is why Jesus said: "Come unto me, all ye that labor and are heavy laden, and I will give you rest"(Matt. 11:28 KJV).

Worship provides restoration and renewal for every serious worker. After seven years of hard labor in working to erect the Temple, a national observance of dedicatory worship provided restoration for a weary nation. Worship in Israel would continue through the centuries to provide the renewal of spirit that the nation would need to face the many challenges that lay ahead of it.

Solomon understood the value of worship, and this was pivotal to his success as a servant of God and as a leader of his people. For Solomon, worship was not optional; it was not something to be done if he felt like it or if he wasn't too tired or if he didn't have anything else to do. Worship was central to Solomon's personal development as well as his public performance. Nothing he did personally or publicly had any eternal significance without the direction, the devotion, and the renewal of worship. Worship was the aim and the culmination of all his endeavors; it provided the impetus for his success as a person and as a public figure. It is only when we come to see our work itself as an act of worship culminating in worship that we gain the ability to stay positive and productive on our jobs.

WORSHIP PROVIDES AN OCCASION FOR NATIONAL UNITY

History reveals a disturbing record of how various religions have been used to fuel dissention, bigotry, violence, and war in the name of God. Religious claims of absolutism and exclusivism, coupled with a strong mandate to proselytize, have wrought havoc in the human community from the dark days of the Crusades to the current religious conflicts in Iraq, Ireland, and Bosnia. Recognizing that religious ideologies are indisputable factors in the escalation of violence and evil around the world, some have suggested that religion itself is the problem. Some pundits argue that religious worldviews are anachronistic and antithetical to the establishment of global cohesion.

The solution to this quandary, however, is not to be found in the wholesale disparagement of all religion. The truth is that there is some religion that hurts and hinders us; and there is some religion that heals and helps us in our quest for human oneness. In its ungrammatical profundity, the lyrics of an old Negro spiritual raise the poignant question, "Is you got good religion?" The question itself begs the acknowledgement that all religion "ain't" necessarily good religion. Some religion can only find truth in its traditions. Other religion finds that truth often transcends tradition and sometimes challenges and changes tradition. Good religion unites us; bad religion divides us. Good religion sees the unconditional love of God for all humanity as the greatest revelation of the Bible; bad religion is fixated upon religious laws that are derived from and limited to the particular cultural perspective of the Biblical writers.

Good religion wakes up every day and says: "Lord lead me into a greater understanding of truth"; bad religion believes that it has already apprehended all truth and therefore has no need to listen and to learn from those of different truth perspectives. Good religion reads the Bible to grow in grace; bad religion reads the Bible to justify its intolerance. Good religion reaches out to bring others in; bad religion closes doors to exclude those who don't fit in. Good religion moves us in the spirit of extravagant welcome; bad religion causes us to practice prejudice in the name of God. Good religion unifies; bad religion polarizes. Some religious people receive the Holy Ghost and become "holier than Thou." Some religious people start speaking in tongues and stop speaking to their neighbors. Some religious people join the church and disconnect themselves from other people in the world whom God loved so much that God gave God's only begotten Son. The question of old is especially pertinent today: "Is you got good religion?"

Not every religious commitment is responsible for the bitter culture wars and moral crusades that blight our planet. In fact, the impetus to reach outside of religious boundaries, catechisms, and traditions in order to fully embrace the whole of humanity without religious stipulation is essentially a religious impetus. For me, it is an impetus based upon the all inclusive love of God incarnated in the person and ministry of Jesus Christ.

In the face of religiosity's potential to damage human solidarity across cultural lines, Solomon provides for us a model for how worship can be used to bring people together instead of tear people apart. Worship gave Solomon the occasion to call his entire nation together for a national convocation. At this convocation, every tribe, every clan, every family of Israel was represented—not one tribe was excluded. Jealousy, competition, and infighting had characterized the twelve tribes of Israel since the progenitors of the nation (the twelve sons of

Jacob) conspired among themselves to sell one of their own brothers into Egyptian slavery.

Dissention and infighting among the twelve tribes would escalate and eventually lead to civil war in Israel, resulting in a divided realm under the imprudent reign of Solomon's son, Rehoboam. Solomon, however, had the wisdom to allow the nation's foundational belief in Yahweh to move the people beyond tribal disputes and call representatives from every tribe together in an awesome display of national unity. Despite the record of confrontations fueled by sectarians, Solomon's national convocation teaches us that religion and worship can still serve the godly goals of national unity.

We should not forget that one of the most religious days in America was September 12, 2001—the day after the attacks of September 11. People across the country made their way to various churches, temples, and mosques in record numbers. Worship in the various cultural arenas throughout the country was conducted in different languages with different expressions, experiences, and designations of the Divine. But in the multiplicity of our conglomerate religious expressions on September 12 and the days that immediately followed, we found a national solidarity and a genuine concern for each other that we have been hard pressed to replicate since those drastic days. It is amazing how God can use human tragedy to build human unity. It is amazing how God can use devastation to shake religion out of the confines of its sanctimonious enclaves, and help religion to rediscover the revelation that at the basis of all faiths there is one God who created and loves all of us—"with partiality toward none" (Acts 10:34).

The thrust of Solomon's national convocation was not to unite Israel against any other nation, culture, or creed. This convocation was not an attempt to establish a civil religion in order to justify nationalistic interests. Solomon's convocation brought the nation together to publicly celebrate the God of their history and to publicly submit to the God of their destiny. In bringing the Arc of the Covenant from Bethlehem to the Temple in Jerusalem, the nation celebrated its sacred heritage. It was a sacred heritage not characterized by military conquests, but by sacred covenant between Yahweh and the nation.

In the prayer that Solomon offered in dedication of the Temple, the nation's submission to and utter dependency upon the mercy of God was the constant refrain. Solomon's national convocation says to us that it is possible to celebrate our history and destiny in God as nation without establishing nationalistic barriers that divide us from other nations. This national convocation teaches us that it is possible to have a religious expression true to the root derivation of religion itself: for the word religion is derived from the Latin root "religio," which means "to bind together." When worship serves the common good instead of parochial agendas, when worship calls us to celebrate our unity in the midst of our diversity, when worship binds us together for a divine purpose that empowers the whole nation instead of commissioning us for crusades against other countries, it plays a vital role in the establishment of national stability and international coexistence. Solomon teaches us that true worship is designed by God to bring all people together across the tribal lines that would divide and destroy us.

Unfortunately for us today, Christendom is becoming more exclusive than inclusive. The Southern Baptist Convention, the largest and wealthiest Christian Protestant denomination in America, has voted to withdraw from the Baptist World Alliance—an international association of Baptists, representing all theological perspectives of the Baptist faith, including conservatives, moderates, and progressives. The religious claims of absolutism and exclusivism continue to motivate the breaking of communion among people in many religious circles. Indeed, the history of the Judeo-Christian faith is a history of the struggles within the church itself toward greater inclusivity.

Solomon and the Jews of his day had not yet spiritually matured to the extent that women could be accepted in the Temple on an equal basis as men. The King James and other versions of the Bible state that only the men who served as elders of the tribes were summoned to the national convocation. Through the centuries, the Judeo-Christian church has continued to struggle with sexist theologies rooted in patriarchy. And for many Christian women, particularly those of Catholic and Baptist persuasion, the struggle against institutional sexism in the church continues.

During the early development of the Christian church in the first century, the Apostle Paul had to fight many bitter battles among his fellow Christians as he proclaimed the full inclusion of noncircumcised Gentile believers into the Judeo-Christian fold. During the 1960s, civil rights activists not only challenged segregation in the body politic, they challenged segregation within the sanctum of American religious institutions.

Dr. Martin Luther King Jr.'s "Letter from the Birmingham Jail" was a direct indictment of white Christian churches in the South for their failure to address the sin of exclusivity and oppression against black people. In his book entitled *Living in Sin,* Bishop John Shelby Spong enumerates other exclusive barriers that the Christian church has historically struggled to overcome:

> All sorts of people were victims of the church's prejudice. Left-handed people were called "the devil's children" by church leaders. People who committed suicide were refused burial from within the walls of the church. Mental illness made people different and, therefore, feared and rejected. Divorced persons who remarried also were not welcome at the church's al-

tars, for the failure to keep one's marriage vows was thought to be an almost unforgivable sin.[2]

The history of the Christian church is indeed the history of Christendom's struggle toward greater inclusiveness. And there are still other barriers to break through. Homophobia remains one of the last "acceptable prejudices" in most Christian churches. Many churches are willing to reinterpret the Levitical abominations against pork and shrimp but refuse to reinvestigate and re-exegete the Levitical abominations ostensibly aimed against same-gender-loving persons.

Many churches can place the cultural perspectives of the Apostle Paul regarding women and slaves in their proper historical context and preach full equality for women and slaves despite the literal reading of Paul's writings in the New Testament. But when it comes to the issue of full inclusion of homosexuals within the body of Christian believers, many churches hold dogmatically to the claims of biblical literalism that were formulated long before any knowledge about the nature and variation of sexual orientation came to be known. The struggle toward greater inclusiveness continues to be the struggle of the Christian church. The absolute claims of biblical literalists have stymied the church's struggles toward inclusiveness, but they have never stopped the struggle.

Every great struggle for progressive social change in America is essentially a religious struggle that must begin with the enlightenment of religious people themselves. Both the judgment and the justice of God begin in the house of God among believers who dare to step out of religious conventions in order to embrace broader revelations of God's universal love. Dr. William Sloane Coffin, former pastor of New York's Riverside Church, succinctly articulates the great challenge facing the Christian church in his book, *A Passion for the Possible:*

> The challenge today is to seek a unity that celebrates diversity, to unite the particular with the universal, to

recognize the need for roots while insisting that the point of roots is to put forth branches. What is intolerable is for difference to become idolatrous. When absolutized, nationalism, ethnicity, race, and gender are reactionary impulses. They become pseudoreligions, brittle and small, without the power to make people great. No human being's identity is exhausted by his or her gender, race, ethnic origin, or national loyalty. Human beings are fully human only when they find the universal in the particular, when they realize that all people have more in common than they have in conflict, and that it is precisely when what they have in conflict seems overriding that what they have in common needs most to be affirmed. Human rights are more important than the politics of identity, and religious people should be notorious boundary crossers.[3]

RELIGIOUS WORSHIP AND PUBLIC POLICY

Though reflective of the patriarchy of his day, Solomon's dedicatory convocation did lay a foundation for bringing people together across tribal lines, and it does serve as a model for discerning the proper role of religion and worship in public affairs. There is much debate today about the role of religion in public policy. There are those who hold so doggedly to the mantra of "separation of church and state" that they reject any interjection of religious belief into the arena of public discourse and decision making.

Opposition to any semblance of a state subsidized religion is understandable. One person's theocracy is another person's religious oppression, because no one religion is normative for everyone. All religion is perceived through the particular experiences and interests of its adherents. Consequently, in order to serve all constituents fairly, public officials of a particular religious tradition must not be bound by those traditions in formulating and administering public policy. Church and state must remain separated in order to protect the integrity of both. Religious organizations must remain free to follow their religious convictions, and the state must remain free to administer justice equitably to all citizens.

While we should support the separation of church and state, we should, however, also acknowledge and allow for the union of faith and public policy. Faith in God does not have to be tied to an allegiance to any one particular church, synagogue or mosque. Faith in God can step outside the perimeters of a particular parish or the dogmatism of a particular denomination to advance transcendent godly principles which serve the whole of humanity—regardless of culture, class or creed. When this kind of faith is brought to bear on public discourse and public policy it serves the well-being of everyone.

Faith that is inclusive of the whole human family allows democracy and equal opportunity to grow in a context of respect for religious diversity. It serves God while at the same time serving the highest good of all the people. It honors God by reaching beyond the constrictions of religious doctrine to include those who are different, dejected, and disenfranchised. It was the inclusive faith of Mahatma Gandhi that inspired him to sacrifice for the liberation of all Indians, including the Buddhists and Muslims.

For that sacrifice, Martin Luther King Jr. called Gandhi the greatest Christian of the twentieth century, though Gandhi was a Hindu. It was the inclusive faith of John F. Kennedy that caused him to reach outside the cloisters of Catholicism to promote the rights of all Americans, including the rights of Protestant African Americans. In 1960, President Kennedy articulated an inclusive religious vision for America:

> I believe in an America where religious intolerance
> will someday end—where all men and all churches

are treated as equal—where every man has the right
to attend or not to attend the church of his choice—
where there is no Catholic vote, no anti-Catholic
vote, no bloc voting of any kind—and where Catho-
lics, Protestants, and Jews, both the lay and the pas-
toral level, will refrain from those attitudes of disdain
and division which have so often marred their works
in the past, and promote instead the American ideal
of brotherhood.[4]

If we understand Kennedy's reference to "man" as being
generically inclusive of men, women, and persons of mixed
gender, if we understand the reference to "churches" as being
inclusive of all faiths, and if we understand the reference to
"brotherhood" as being inclusive of the whole human community, then I believe that this vision still serves as a guideline
to religious and moral discourse in America today.

There is no doubt that the doctrine of separation between church and state is vital to the civil liberties and religious freedoms of a democratic society. However, the separation of church and state does not mean the separation of
moral values from public policy. The presidential election of
2004 taught us that American voters will not divorce politics
from morality—and no one should expect otherwise. Most
American voters are motivated, at least ostensibly, by some
form of moral mandate, which is usually derived from some
kind of religious perspective. In fact, the 2004 election has
shown us that persons can even be persuaded to ignore and
to vote against their own economic and political interests, if
they view the moral issues as compelling enough.

In his incisive book entitled *God's Politics,* Jim Wallis asks:
"Since when did believing in God and having moral values
make you pro-war, pro-rich, and pro-Republican? And since
when did promoting and pursuing a progressive social
agenda with a concern for economic security, health care, and

educational opportunity mean you had to put faith in God aside?"[5] Wallis goes on to say:

> While the Right in America has hijacked the language of faith to prop up its political agenda—an agenda not all people of faith support—the Left hasn't done much better, largely ignoring faith and continually separating moral discourse and personal ethics from public policy. While the Right argues that God's way is their way, the Left pursues an unrealistic separation of religious values from morally grounded political leadership. The consequence is a false choice between ideological religion and soulless politics.[6]

The venerable Rev. Dr. Joseph E. Lowery contends that people of faith—Christians in particular—are dealing with a case of identity theft. He says that the true identity of Jesus has been stolen by hard-line conservatives, to the extent that Jesus no longer resembles the loving, serving, humble, compassionate peacemaker that he was. Dr. Lowery challenges authentic Christians and progressive people of faith to recover and reclaim the true identity of Christ for the salvation of the world.[7]

Political progressives cannot afford to ignore the vital significance of religious and moral values in the debates over public policy. We must insist, however, that the morality of public policy not be dictated by the dogma or doctrine of any one religion or theological perspective. Progressives must never forget that in the vanguard of the civil rights movement, which transformed the segregationist structures and racist ethos of American society, there were Christian and Jewish clergy persons, whose religious commitments inspired them to embrace justice for all Americans, without regard to color, class, or creed. Progressives must rediscover and reclaim the moral footing of our political engagement. We must steadfastly proclaim again and again that tolerance and respect for diversity are also moral values. In fact, they are the critical moral values needed to keep a pluralistic society intact and a true democracy vibrant. Based upon the gospel of the Bible itself, we must proclaim with religious fervor that the most un–Christ-like thing to do is to practice intolerance of persons from other religious and cultural persuasions. As religious people grounded in moral truth, we must insist upon moral principles that transcend parochial catechisms and moral values that transcend religious affiliations.

And we must do all of this in the spirit of the Nazarean prophet who proclaimed to his followers: "I have other sheep that do not belong to this fold. I must bring them also." (John 10:16). It will not be until the "other sheep" are respected, affirmed, and valued; not until the "other sheep" from God's other folds—from other perspectives, other cultures, other religions, other ethnicities, other revelations, other philosophies, and other sexual orientations—are able to coexist with the sheep from your fold and the sheep from my fold that the Great Shepherd of every fold on the planet will be glorified. We must choose now between coexistence or nonexistence. This is the pressing moral issue of our day that progressives must help to define. Tolerance and respect for diversity are essential religious values among any people, and they must never be co-opted or compromised by the myopia of religious claims of absolutism. God must love diversity; that's why she made so much of it.

Political progressives in the United States have done a serious disservice to their own cause by voiding religious conviction from their political engagements. It is the common perception that progressives have lost the national debate about moral values to the conservatives. However, if conservatives have won the debate on moral values in America, it is precisely because in recent years progressives have been reluctant to fully engage the debate.

Progressives have basically ceded the language of moral values to the conservatives. Concerning the moral issue of abortion, progressives have been reluctant to make the moral claim that if it is absolutely wrong to kill a person before he or she is born, then it must also be absolutely wrong to kill a person after he or she is born, which makes conservative support for capital punishment and the National Rifle Association morally inconsistent and indefensible. Furthermore, to be pro-choice is not necessarily to be pro-abortion, and choice itself is a moral value offered to everyone by God: "Choose you this day whom you will serve" (Josh. 24:15 KJV). When religion usurps a person's right to choose, it violates an inherent gift from our Creator and mistakenly presumes that righteousness is a byproduct of moral coercion.

Progressives can further question whether or not it is more morally objectionable to kill a potential child before birth by abortion or to kill a child after birth by aborting public funds for low income child care, public education, the eradication of slums, affirmative action, diversity scholarships, job opportunities, and a national health care insurance program. Progressives have the right to argue that the national budget itself is a moral document that does not reflect the love of Jesus if it is devoid of adequate funding to care for the indigent and the disenfranchised—those whom Jesus called "the least of these" (Matt. 25:40 KJV).

Progressives should not sidestep the moral issue of gay marriage. The religious rite of marriage has never been challenged. It is expected that every religious institution will administer marriage rites according to its respective religious convictions. However, marriage also carries with it certain civil rights, and it is immoral to deny the civil rights of any citizen based upon religious or cultural bias. Those who would seek to codify discrimination against anyone into the United States Constitution serve to establish an immoral and unjust precedent that can only jeopardize the civil rights of all marginalized in groups. A threat to justice anywhere is indeed a threat to justice everywhere.

Religious and cultural bias against the civil marriage of two responsible adults legally prevented blacks from marrying blacks and blacks from marrying whites in certain states in America for decades. Progressives should press the case that those civil marriage restrictions were wrong then and they are wrong now. Prejudice, even when it enjoys religious sanction, is not a family value. The traditional American family unit will always be valued, but it is wrong to discount and dismiss those who do not fit into that traditional paradigm. The concept of extended family does not negate the traditional family unit; it simply does not limit the definition of family or family values to the traditional Euro-American conservative model. The concept of extended family is the only real bedrock upon which a healthy society can be built because the extended family model leaves no one outside the family. The extended family connects each of us together in a single garment of mutuality, humanity, and destiny by making each of us our brother's and our sister's keeper.

The truth is that families have always come in various configurations. A picture of Abraham's family would not only include his wife Sarah and their son Isaac; it would also include Hagar and their son Ishmael, who were also remembered and blessed by God. A picture of Ruth's family would not just include her husband Boaz; it would also include her mother-in-law Naomi—the woman Ruth vowed never to leave and the woman for whom Ruth bore a child, according to Ruth 4:13–15. A picture of the psalmist David's family would certainly not be complete without Jonathan and Jonathan's descendents, whom David took care of because of his deeply abiding love for Jonathan. A picture of the Apostle Paul's family could include Silas, Barnabus, Luke, and Onesimus—the slave turned brother who ministered to Paul while Paul ministered to others.

From a moral and biblical basis, as well as in the arena of public policy, progressives have a moral basis to argue that families come in all configurations. On one occasion, Mother Mary and the brothers of Jesus stood outside a house where Jesus was ministering, requesting Jesus to come out to them. But Jesus transcended the traditional model of his own family and gave us the true definition of family when, instead of going outside the house to join his conventional family, Jesus looked around at the people in the crowded house where he was, and then raised the critical question, "Who is my mother? And who are my brothers?"

According to Mark 3:34–35, Jesus, while looking at those around him, said, "Whosoever [Anybody] who does the will of God is my brother and my sister and my mother." It is a travesty of Jesus' teaching and a travesty of justice to deny equal rights to anyone in the family of Jesus based upon a truncated concept of traditional family values. The family of Jesus is as broad as the whole of humanity and is as strong as the ties that bind our hearts together in love. Progressives need not eschew this moral issue nor genuflect to the moral majority/Christian Coalition. We can lift up the family values of Jesus as our definitive moral paradigm.

We must not miss the fact that many of the religious and political conservatives who see it as their sacred duty to counsel the nation on "family values'" have done much to destroy families. In 2005, conservatives in the Georgia state legislature passed one of the most restrictive pieces of voting legislation in recent history. The legislation, House Bill 244, effectively limited the forms of identification voters could use to six and also required photo identification. This voter restriction was an assault upon the enfranchisement of the elderly, African Americans, the poor, and black students who attend the private colleges and universities of the Atlanta University Center. Despite the fact that the major instances of voter fraud occurred by absentee ballot and that an absentee vote requires absolutely no identification, Georgia conservative lawmakers left absentee voting completely intact. In March of

2005, the voting rights of thousands of marginalized families in Georgia were severely restricted by the majority of representatives and senators in the Georgia legislature. On the next day, those same legislators held a "Family Day" at the state capitol to display their support of families in Georgia. This sanctimonious promotion of "family values" by those who obviously do not respect all families is, in my estimation, disingenuous and morally reprehensible. The family of Jesus is big enough to incorporate the whole of humanity. "Family values" that are skewed in favor of some families to the exclusion of others cannot truly reflect the kinship of Christ. Progressives must not eschew the moral debate.

WORSHIP AS THE DIVINE COMMON DENOMINATOR

At the national convocation of worship and dedication, Solomon and the entire congregation of Israel stood before the Ark of the Covenant in the newly erected Temple, sacrificing sheep and cattle in praise and supplication to Almighty God. In thanksgiving and in repentance, Solomon and all the people offered countless sacrifices unto God. In their sacrificial offerings, Solomon and all the people acknowledged their sinfulness before the presence of God. Not one tribe, family, or individual, including King Solomon himself, was exempted or excluded from the need to offer sacrifices to God in repentance for sins committed. The people came from different tribes, but all of them, including King Solomon, shared a common condition of unrighteousness as they stood before the supernal excellency of God's presence in the Temple.

Worship provided for the people the opportunity to strip away tribal and class distinctions in order to find their common identity as children of God who were all dependent upon God's grace and mercy. True worship does not justify some and condemn others. True worship strips away our social badges of distinction and removes our religious classifications so that we can all see our common condition as imperfect sinners dependent upon the mercy and grace of Almighty God. No one is excluded or exempted from the religious mandate to repent.

From the ruler to the common laborers; from the prestigious nobility to the obscure farm laborers; from the high priests to the lowly beggars—all the people found their common identity as sinners and their common dependency upon God's mercy, in worship. Some of us may judge ourselves to be better than the rest of us, but when we all stand before the excellence of God's judgment, every one of us is found deficient. In contradistinction to our selective social systems and religious hierarchies, God is no respecter of persons.

From the penthouse to the poor house; from the White House to the "out house"; from the well-heeled to the homeless; from the palace to the projects; from the highly educated to the long-term incarcerated—all have sinned and come short of the glory of God (Rom. 3:23). Worship should bring everyone closer together in unity and solidarity, because worship reveals our common condition of sinfulness and our common hope of redemption through faith in our common Creator/Redeemer. This is the fundamental truth that can rescue worship from becoming a pompous display of religious arrogance and instead provide a renewed impetus for a collective consciousness of human humility. Imagine a nationwide call to worship in American that would unite all of us in our common identity as God's children and humble all of us in our common dependency upon God's mercy.

Imagine a nationwide call to worship in America that would allow us to celebrate our oneness as a people while promoting malice toward no other nation. Imagine a nationwide call to worship in America that could cut through the hierarchies and distinctions of class, race, and culture and offer persons from every tribal affiliation a place in the sacred assembly of the Divine. In the classic song "Imagine," John

Lennon of Beatles fame imagined a world that would not be divided by bellicose nationalism and sectarian religious ideology. In keeping with Lennon's exquisite vision of worldwide oneness, I imagine a world that could be united by national identities that are informed by global consciousness and by religious convictions that celebrate divine unity through human diversity.

QUESTIONS FOR REFLECTION

1. What are the long- and short-term effects of work without worship? How do you relate your work to your worship?

2. How have you seen worship used to unite or divide people?

3. Discuss your understanding of moral values and public policy in light of the mantra to keep church and state separate.

4. What are some moral issues about which you think progressive Christians have been too silent?

4

THE FOURTH KEY: WITNESS

1 Kings 10:1–9 (NIV)

1 When the Queen of Sheba heard about the fame of Solomon and his relation to the name of God, she came to test him with hard questions.

2 Arriving at Jerusalem with a very great caravan—with camels carrying spices, large quantities of gold, and precious stones—she came to Solomon and talked with him about all that she had on her mind.

3 Solomon answered all her questions; nothing was too hard for the king to explain to her.

4 When the Queen of Sheba saw all the wisdom of Solomon and the palace he had built,

5 the food on his table, the seating of his officials, the attending servants in their robes, his cupbearers, and the burnt offerings he made at the temple of God, she was overwhelmed.

6 She said to the king, "The report I heard in my own country about your achievements and your wisdom is true.

7 But I did not believe these things until I came and saw with my own eyes. Indeed, not even half was told me; in wisdom and wealth you have far exceeded the report I heard.

8 How happy your men must be! How happy your officials, who continually stand before you and hear your wisdom!

9 Praise be to your Sovereign God, who has delighted in you
and placed you on the throne of Israel. Because of God's
eternal love for Israel, God has made you king, to maintain
justice and righteousness."

THE INTENT OF OUR WITNESS

Many persons have mistaken Christian witness for Christian
coercion. Many Christian believers are under the mistaken
impression that in order to share their faith, they must subscribe to intense formulas for Christian proselytization. Most
Christians have engaged in or been confronted by zealous
evangelists and "heaven or hell" tracts designed to convert or
condemn us for eternity. What many of us in our evangelistic
zeal do not comprehend is that the power of our witness is
not in our power to proselytize.

The power of our witness is in our ability to share our experience of God with integrity and then allow people to make
their own decisions, even as they affirm their own experiences
with God. We make a mistake when we assume that through
our evangelistic endeavors we bring God or Christ into anyone's life. Many European missionaries assumed that they
brought Christianity to "the dark continent" of Africa when
they went there to Christianize and to colonize. Most of
them had no regard for the rich spirituality of indigenous
African people, which was expressed through ancestral
shrines and icons.

Indigenous Africans understood the Christian concept of
"the great cloud of witnesses" (Heb. 12:1) long before
European Christian missionaries came to convert and colonize
them. African theologians argue that the theological concept
of monotheism or universal Spirit was not a concept that had
to be imported to Africa. Indeed, the African Coptic Church

itself had long established an indigenous Christian identity in Africa before the entrenchment of European missionaries.

According to the second chapter of Acts, the power of the Holy Spirit was revealed to persons from every nation at the same time. The point here is that our witness as believers has less to do with our power to convert others and much more to do with our opportunity to open up lines of spiritual communication. The sincere expression of our experience with the Divine through love and integrity translates into a dialogical religious exchange that can be respected around the world. When our evangelistic aim shifts from indoctrination to engagement, from coercion to communication, then the appeal of our witness can emerge. It was not in Solomon's intent to proselytize, but in his willingness to share his faith with integrity, that he discovered the power of his witness.

THE APPEAL OF OUR WITNESS

The Queen of Sheba did not share Solomon's ethnicity, culture, or faith, but she heard that there was a king in Israel who was all about excellence in the way he lived, in the words he spoke, in the manner in which he governed his people, and in the international coalitions he had established. And so she determined that she would take the fifteen-hundred-mile journey across the arid sands of the Arabian desert to meet him for herself. The region of Sheba was located in southwestern Arabia—Ethiopia—also known as ancient Nubia, which is a part of northwestern Africa. In Matthew 12:42, Jesus refers to her as the "Queen of the South." The Queen of Sheba was a beautiful, wealthy, African monarch in her own right. Yet, notwithstanding her own prominence, power, and privilege, she still found something appealing in Solomon's reputation of wisdom and wealth. She had no material needs, and she apparently sought no greater levels of political power or personal fame. What she did have was a series of questions about life, about love, about wisdom, about God, about death, and about eternity that her wealth and prestige could not answer.

She had heard that Solomon was not only wealthy but wise. She had heard that Solomon not only possessed the fine materials of life, but that he also possessed wisdom for discerning the finer meanings of life. She had heard that Solomon was not only monetarily endowed but spiritually insightful. Much more than the appeal of wealth, it was the appeal of wisdom that drew the Queen of Sheba to Solomon. She came not primarily to behold his wealth, but to test his wisdom with some hard questions.

Many people today are drawn to the church for the same reason that the Queen of Sheba was drawn to King Solomon. People today are wrestling with some hard questions. They are questions that cannot be answered by money and material, questions that cut across income brackets, educational attainments, professional merits, and class distinctions. They are questions that cannot be answered by euphemistic homilies, religious platitudes or cursory readings of the Bible. They are questions that call for critical thinking, deep discernment, and insightful reasoning. Critical thinking and insightful inquiry are in serious jeopardy among many contemporary Christians.

The prevailing marketing strategy for megachurch appeal dictates that controversial issues either be avoided or definitively settled by the proclamation (not necessarily the explanation) of conventional religious doctrine. In many religious settings, no further inquiry, investigation, or discussion is permitted beyond the conventional mantra of the established religious doctrine. The current multimillion dollar Christian entertainment industry has capitalized on this marketing strategy. Most Christian mega-entertainment centers are not places where people feel comfortable questioning the meaning, relevance, and pertinent truth of established religious doctrines and religious institutional structures. Many believers do not even see critical thinking and insightful judgment as necessary aspects of our worship and walk with God. Because we find our spiritual security in numbers and we define our discipleship by our blind acquiescence to the religious status quo, we are reluctant to raise the hard questions in our religious settings.

But just because hard questions are not raised does not mean that they do not exist in the hearts and minds of many people. Like the Queen of Sheba, we have all the trappings of superficial success and we can recite all the catechisms of conventional religion, but in the deeper recesses of our consciousness we are still wrestling with some hard questions. Hard questions like: Since the Bible says that whatever things you ask for in prayer, believe that you have received it, and it will be yours (Mark. 11:24), then why do I keep believing and praying, but receiving nothing I pray for? Hard questions like: Since the Bible says it is better to marry than to burn, is it wise for me to get married in order to assuage my conscience about having sex with the one that sets my passions aflame?

Hard questions like: if one of God's Ten Commandments is "Thou shall not kill," then why did God direct the Levites to go through their encampment at Sinai and slay three thousand of their brothers, friends, and neighbors (Exod. 32:27)? Does that divine directive give us the right to kill those whom we deem to be enemies of God? Hard questions like: If God wants me to tithe or give the church ten percent of my income, then why do I barely make enough money to pay my bills? Hard questions like: If God hates divorce, does that mean that I am supposed to spend the rest of my life in a loveless, abusive marriage? Hard questions like: If it is wrong to be a homosexual, then why are so many God-fearing people, by their own testimony and by the preponderance of scientific evidence, born that way?

Hard questions like: Since the Bible says that the prayer of faith will save the sick and God will raise them up, why do so many faithful, praying Christians get sick and die? Hard questions like: If Christianity is the only true religion, does that mean that Muslims, Jews, Buddhists, and all other non-Christian people around the world are bound for hell and eternal damnation?

Hard questions like: If the theories of evolution are absolutely false and the story of the creation in Genesis is absolutely true as it is written, then how did the two sons of Adam and Eve have children unless they committed incest with their own mother? Hard questions like: If God is good, and if God is omnipotent, why does evil exist? Hard questions like: Can I believe that the Bible is the Word of God and still not believe that every word or expression in the Bible is an infallible revelation of God's truth?

Hard questions like: Is assisted suicide ever justifiable in the face of prolonged suffering and expressed desires to die? Hard questions like: Is it permissible to use human embryos for stem cell research in order to prolong and improve the lives of those who suffer with chronic illnesses? Hard questions like: If we can't believe in everything the Bible says, can we believe in anything the Bible says? These are just a few of the many, many hard questions that people live with every day. The disallowance of critical Bible study, in-depth investigation, and candid discussion concerning these matters will not make them go away.

THE WITNESS OF OPEN DIALOGUE AND CRITICAL DISCUSSION

Relevant religion cannot circumvent the hard questions of life through high praise or emotional appeals to religious tradition. The true witness of Solomon is that his faith was strong enough and real enough to engage the hard questions. Solomon could have stopped the queen at the outset of her inquiry by saying to her: "We don't question God here, we just believe!" Solomon could have cut her off at the very beginning by saying: "We don't question our religious traditions, we just follow them." Solomon could have avoided her questions by quoting some Scriptures and telling her: "We don't question the Bible, we just believe in it." But instead, Solomon engaged her skepticism, welcomed her investigation, and addressed all her hard questions in open, honest, critical, candid dialogue.

The Bible says that Solomon answered all of her questions and that nothing was too hard for him to explain to her. He did not avoid her questions by hiding behind unexamined Scripture and religious jargon. He answered all her questions. Not one question was too hard. Not one question was too taboo. Not one question was too secular. Not one question was too strange or too unusual that it could not be addressed and answered by the wisdom of God. What a witness for God's realm. If the church today is going to have any credible witness among critical thinkers, the church will have to abandon its allegiance to blind faith and engage people where they are by addressing the hard questions.

The renowned orator and theologian Dr. Gardner Taylor has predicted that the megachurch movement will soon discover that the real issues of life defy easy answers. Most often, life mirrors the game show "Jeopardy." Our greatest points of discovery are not always in the revelation of the right answers, but in the formulation of the right questions. Indeed, sometimes our questions are even more challenging and revealing than our answers. Solomon's great witness was evidenced in his willingness to engage the hard questions.

THE WITNESS OF PERSONAL DEDICATION

Solomon's witness was not just limited to dialogue and discussion. Solomon's witness was also reflective of his personal dedication to excellence and integrity. After Solomon and the queen dialogued openly, the queen then observed intensely.

She looked around carefully, no doubt to see if there would be any correlation between Solomon's words and Solomon's deeds. We know how easy it is to talk a good game, but after our conversations, what does a close inspection of our lives really reveal? Is there really any correlation and consistency between what we say and how we actually live?

Our wisdom is not just in the directives we give to others; our wisdom is evidenced in our willingness and in our ability to follow our own advice and live according to our own truth. After the Queen of Sheba had heard everything Solomon had to say, she looked around and paid close attention to see if Solomon's wisdom actually bore any fruit in Solomon's own household. The critical question for those of us who are leaders is, does our public witness have any bearing on the way we live at home? Can our public testimonies withstand the scrutiny of personal investigation? Are we talking peace publicly but raising hell at home?

Are we advocating for global unity but refusing to compromise with the people in our own neighborhood? Are we advising others to forgive their detractors but refusing to forgive those who personally trespass against us? Are we extolling the virtues of agape abroad but failing to love unconditionally those who abide in our own personal spheres? The Queen of Sheba heard what Solomon had to say. She then looked carefully around the house that Solomon had built, to determine if his personal deeds matched his public creeds. What the Queen of Sheba saw was not only a house that was well constructed; she saw a household that was well constituted, well organized, and well integrated. She saw that Solomon had not only built a house, she saw that Solomon had built a home. She saw that Solomon exhibited not only public wisdom but personal integrity.

The Queen of Sheba looked around and observed the food on Solomon's table. Perhaps she was looking to see what kind of food does a person of such great wisdom ingest?

What a person ingests, not just physically, but spiritually and intellectually, reveals a great deal about a person's character and aptitude. There is usually much on our tables to feed our bodies and our sensual passions, but is there anything on our tables to feed our minds and our spirits? Are there any great books or ideas on our tables to sustain our souls and renew our minds? When was the last time we connected and reflected upon a noble idea through reading a book? When was the last time we turned off our televisions and awakened our dormant imagination on a vicarious adventure provided to us via a good novel? Or does our literary diet merely consist of the junk food of the tabloids or the mundane statistics of the sports pages?

Is there any meat on our tables to help us to understand more of the Bible's message, meaning, and compilation? Is there any meat on our tables to connect us with persons who live outside of our cultural niche? Is there any meat on the table to help us become better caretakers of our bodies and better stewards of our financial resources? Is there any meat on the table to enable us to better control the stresses of our varied emotions and to avoid the toxicities of our polluted environment? Is there any meat on the table to help us understand how to build loving relationships that last? Is there any meat on our table to help us become more informed participants in the democratic processes of government? Is there any meat on our tables to enable us to relate better to our children and/or our parents? Is there any meat on our tables for the development of our minds and the broadening of our perspectives? The Queen of Sheba took careful note of what was on Solomon's table. She paid close attention to what he ingested.

Then the queen looked at the organization and the order of Solomon's household. She noticed the high decorum and the careful organization evidenced in the seating of Solomon's officials—everyone was in place. She noticed the high level of efficiency and attentiveness that characterized Solomon's servants and cup bearers. She noticed that everyone in Solomon's court knew and performed his or her responsibilities with exacting proficiency. No one was out of step or out of sync. Not one attention to detail was neglected. Everyone was in proper uniform, attire, and attitude. Every component of gracious hospitality was displayed. Every courtesy was extended. Unity, efficiency, and cohesion permeated the palace.

The Queen of Sheba kept looking around, kept observing, kept taking mental notes on everything she saw. And the more she saw, the more impressed she became. The more she observed, the more her spirit was moved. In my mind's eye, I see the queen and King Solomon reclining gracefully on the lavish veranda of Solomon's sprawling royal estate. Servants stand nearby ready to attend to the slightest whim, while others fan zephyr breezes gently in the direction of the king and his distinguished guest as they sip sweet nectar and look coquettishly into one another's eyes. Melodic music from the harp soothes their senses and sweet-smelling exotic spices perfume the air while candles flicker to illuminate the opulence and flowery, ornate design of the palatial gardens.

Copious platters of exquisite cuisine are paraded and placed before them as golden goblets of fine wine are filled and refilled without request. Then, at some point, in the midst of this grand spectacle of splendor, I see Solomon get up from the cushioned comfort of his royal sofa and say to the queen: "I know you came here to check me out. I know you came to see if all that you've heard about me is really true. I know you came to test me with hard questions and conduct a personal investigation of my character. But if you really want to know the source of my wisdom; if you really want to know the source of my strength and the key to my success; if you really want to know what motivates, inspires, and empowers me to be who I am and to accomplish what I have accomplished, then, your Highness, we're going to have to leave my house and go up into the God's house.

"For you must understand that all of my wisdom, all of my work, all of my witness, all my accomplishments, all of my success, and all of my help comes from God!" Then King Solomon ushered the Queen of Sheba into the Temple, where she observed him offering praise and sacrificing burnt offerings to the glory of the Most High God.

THE WITNESS OF PERSONAL TESTIMONY

It is precisely our willingness to engage (not judge) people where they are and our dedication to personal and professional excellence that opens the door of opportunity for us to share our faith with others. The Queen of Sheba was not initially impressed by Solomon's religion. She was initially impressed by how Solomon's religion empowered him to become such a wise leader and such a person of high integrity. It was only after Solomon manifested the effects of his faith that he then found an appropriate segue to share the essence of his faith.

Jesus, himself, recommended the effects of the Christian faith over the doctrines of the Christian faith when he told his disciples: "By this everyone will know that you are my disciples, if you have love for one another" (John 13:35). It is the manifested fruit of the gospel, not the doctrinal claims of the gospel that opens people's hearts to a serious consideration of the gospel. The Queen of Sheba was moved by the effects of Solomon's faith before she even found out the essence of Solomon's faith. It was the fruit of Solomon's faith that motivated her to go with him to the Temple and investigate the faith itself.

Likewise, our personal testimonies of the Judeo-Christian faith must include much more than our sanctimonious insistence on the truth of our religious claims. Our personal testimonies of the Judeo-Christian faith must include a demonstrated commitment to excellence in the wisdom of our public pronouncements, the justice of our public policies, the efficiency of our professional operations, and the integrity of our personal pursuits. Revivals, evangelistic crusades, and missionary expeditions alone will not be enough to convince a skeptical world that the love of God is enlightenment and empowerment for everyone. The message of the gospel must be incarnated and demonstrated in the public institutions as well as the personal affairs of people who claim to know the way of salvation.

By the time she was invited to the Temple to worship with Solomon, the Queen of Sheba had already been convinced that Solomon's wisdom was genuine, his work was effective and his witness was sincere. A husband and wife duet called the Consolers had a popular gospel song some years ago with lyrics that said: "May the life I live speak for me. May the service I give speak for me." Solomon's life and service spoke volumes about his faith before he ushered the Queen of Sheba into the Temple.

When the Queen of Sheba had experienced and inspected the wonderful wisdom, work, witness, and worship of King Solomon, she was deeply moved. She was cut to the core of her being. She dropped all of her defenses. She opened her heart and her mind to a new and different experience of the Divine. She broadened her faith to accept the value and the virtue of a faith that she had not previously known. She became willing to step outside of her own culture to embrace a faith that she found to be real. She was overwhelmed by the magnanimity of God's goodness and grace personified in King Solomon and manifested through his service.

When the queen beheld and imbibed all of that, the King James Version says: "There was no more spirit in her," indicating the total abandonment of her resistance to Jehovah's loving embrace. Is not this mode of faith witness infinitely more valuable than religious manipulation and indoctrination? The Queen of Sheba came to meet Solomon; she ended up being introduced to the God of Israel. She came to observe Solomon's work; she ended up with Solomon in worship. She came to investigate Solomon's house; she ended up in God's house. She came with her mind on the man; she departed with her mind on God. She said to Solomon, after experiencing his wisdom, his work, his witness, and his worship: "The report I heard in my own country about your wisdom and your achievements is true. But I did not believe these things until I came and saw with my own eyes. Now I know for myself that not even the half was told."

I believe that if you can tell everything you know, you don't know much. If you can explain everything you feel, you don't feel much; and if you can articulate everything you have, you don't have much. Our experience of God is so wide and so deep and so vast that we simply cannot tell it all. The absolute definitive Word of God cannot be contained in a book or expressed in a doctrine, for God is always infinitely more than anything we could ever think, believe, or imagine.

Even when we think we've heard it all, God is speaking. For me, the excitement of my witness for God is not in my ability to relate all of God's truth to an individual. It is rather in my invitation to an individual to experience God for him- or herself. I believe that when a person experiences God authentically, he or she will not come away with compact doctrines and definitive religious assertions. That person will be left with the wondrous testimony of the queen who exclaimed: "The half has not been told."

Without condemning her faith, Solomon caused the Queen of Sheba to consider, respect, and embrace the faith of Israel. The queen proclaimed to Solomon: "Praise be to your Sovereign God, who has delighted in you and placed you on the throne of Israel. Because of God's eternal love for Israel, God has made you king to maintain justice and righteousness" (1 Kgs 10:9 NIV).

Justice and righteousness make for a strong appeal in any culture. Together they form a universal language that any person can respect. The keys to Solomon's success were derived from his faithful focus upon his personal righteous integrity and his commitment to execute justice for all his people. At the outset of his career, he was wise enough to look beyond the mandates of his own personal aggrandizement and petition God for the wisdom to govern his people with sincere righteousness and discerning justice. God granted Solomon's request and blessed him beyond measure. In the process of delivering righteous justice to his own people, Solomon was able reach beyond his own borders and empower other nations with purposeful employment and just compensation. The wisdom of Solomon continues to hold the keys to success for those of us who endeavor to lead God's people today. The keys are so simple, yet so profound. The keys are still available and they are still effective. With them, we can unlock the doors to personal fulfillment, national healing, and universal human solidarity. To God be the glory!

RELIGIOUS WITNESS FOR WORLDWIDE UNITY

With the ever-increasing realities of global interdependence, the need for a religious perspective that is respectful and inclusive of different faith traditions is essential to the peace of the planet. Arguably, religious conflict is one of, if not the greatest, contributor to national and international unrest. Solomon's openness to dialogue and collaboration with persons who were clearly outside of his faith tradition gives us inspiration toward greater ecumenism and interreligious dialogue. In this post–September 11, 2001, era, it behooves all persons of faith to respect and learn about various faith traditions. Those of us who are committed to the ideal of one world under one God, however, will find that the path to interreligious dialogue and collaboration is laden with religious peril. A "religion of inclusion" that proclaims that the love and affirmation of God are not limited to any religion, culture, or sexual orientation is not acceptable or profitable in most religious circles. It is the absolutist claims of most religious adherents that mitigates against the development of a worldwide interfaith community of mutual respect and collaboration.

For many years, Bishop Carlton Pearson of Tulsa, Oklahoma, enjoyed the status of an evangelical superstar. President Bush invited him to the White House. He was a regularly featured guest of the Trinity Broadcasting Network (a national evangelical cable channel), he routinely appeared in national Christian publications, he was a beloved son of his alma mater, Oral Roberts University, and he pastored the five-thousand-member Higher Dimensions Family Church. When Carlton Pearson began preaching a "gospel of inclusion" about four years ago, all of that changed.

Bishop Pearson says that 90 percent of his five-thousand-member congregation in Tulsa has left him. His church is now in foreclosure. Oral Roberts University has publicly denounced him, and long-time colleagues in ministry have ostracized him.[1] This is but one acute example of the religious intolerance rampant in evangelical circles.

In my own Victory Church of Stone Mountain, Georgia, twenty-five hundred members left our congregation in protest of my preaching the love and affirmation of God for homosexuals as well as heterosexuals. Many of the twenty-five hundred who departed were strong financial supporters. Theological messages that extol the religious traditions of exclusivist moral absolutism are clearly the order of the day. Literal interpretations of Scripture, which do not challenge believers to "rightly divide the Word," or to think critically about the text, or to carefully discern the differences between eternal truth and cultural convention in the Bible, are popular and easily digestible.

Persons who dare to preach and believe that God's love and affirmation is extended to anyone outside of the traditional religious rubric of righteousness will often face the scorn of their own religious institutions.

The real question is how can one accept the legitimacy of other faiths without betraying the doctrine's of one's own? Is the call for religious tolerance tantamount to a dilution of one's own religious convictions? Does religious intolerance equate to no religious identity at all? Perhaps Christians should remember that Jesus never distinguished himself by his doctrine, but by his deeds. In fact, it was often his radical deeds of inclusive love, which he extended to many who were outside the boundaries of his religious tradition, that won him the "righteous" indignation of his fellow Jewish dogmatists.

Jesus reached out and changed the lives of people through universal love, not through Jewish law. Consequently, to confess belief in Jesus does not necessarily limit the Christian faith to the person of Jesus, but instead grounds the Christian faith in God's universal love personified in Jesus. The person of Jesus speaks of a cultural identity. The personification of God in Jesus speaks of universal love.

Instead of blurring the distinctiveness of one's religion, an appreciation for religious tolerance could in fact allow a religious person to more accurately compare and contrast his or her religion with other religions of the world in such a way that one's particular religious convictions are enhanced. To believe that God is revealed in one's religion is not necessarily to believe that God's revelation is absent from all other religions. Huston Smith, a noted scholar in comparative religions, stays true to his Christian faith by adhering to the adage: "God is defined by Jesus but is not confined to Jesus." His lifelong study of religion has led him to become a Christian universalist, who believes that God is revealed in many religions. He goes on to say that "Christianity has been from the very start my meal, but I'm a strong believer in vitamin supplements."²

My own Christian conviction is similar to that of Huston Smith. As a Christian, I believe that Jesus Christ is the highest revelation of God, but not the only revelation of God. I compare Jesus, the *son* of God to the *sun* of our universe. The sun never needs to compete with other lights, including the lights of other stars or the lights generated by electricity.

The sun is the greatest light in the our solar system by virtue of its energy and by virtue of its function in creating and maintaining life and balance. The sun does not need a campaign or a crusade to prove its importance or its preeminence. All it has to do is shine. All other lights in the solar system, both natural and electric, can shine simultaneously with the sun and can provide illumination for the sustenance of places and peoples. But no matter how many other lights shine, every light and every life is touched by the light of the sun. The sun does not need to proclaim absolute light unto itself.

The sun does not need to argue with other lights about which light is greater. All the sun has to do is shine. I am convinced that all Christians really have to do is let our light of love and peace shine throughout the world, not to compete or to outshine anyone else's light, but to illuminate every dark space of hatred and neglect, so that the universal creation can live together in the all encompassing illumination of universal love. God is love, and love can no more be completely contained by any one religion than the light of the sun can be completely captured by any one dimension of the solar system. The love of God in Christ Jesus is far too magnanimous to be contained by Christians alone.

Bruce Feiler, best-selling author of *Abraham: A Journey to the Heart of Three Faiths,* contends that most sacred texts, including the Bible and the Koran, are filled with passages that encourage an inclusive view of faith. He goes on to note that these sacred texts contain much that has been borrowed and quoted from other faith traditions.[3] Stories of a great flood appeared in several ancient religious texts, not just the Old Testament. The Christian halo, depicted in Christian art, was borrowed from the ancient Persian religion of Zoroastrianism. Even the premiere Christian evangelist of the New Testament, the Apostle Paul, borrowed from prevailing Greek poets and philosophers of his day to promote his gospel of Christ. "The God who made the world and everything in it . . ." (Acts 17:24)—that is language straight out of Greek Stoic philosophy. And later Paul says, "In him we live and move and have our being" (Acts 17:28); that is a quotation from a Greek philosopher named Epimenides. And "For we too are his offspring" (Acts 17:28) is a line from a well-known Greek poet, Aratus. The cross-fertilization of various religious themes and philosophies in sacred canons themselves gives impetus to greater interreligious dialogue and understanding.

Solomon's understanding of his faith did not lead him into the isolation of religious absolutism. Instead, it enabled him to build bridges of religious dialogue, economic collaboration, and cultural exchange with many persons outside of his faith tradition. The religion of Judaism was fortified for the Jews and respected by other faith traditions because of Solomon's openness to diversity.

While some could argue that it was precisely Solomon's openness to the religious diversity of his many wives that caused his eventual demise, I would contend that it was not his openness to others, but his failure to respect and uphold the values of his own faith that caused his decline. Solomon lost sight of his faithfulness to God through his commitment to serve his people, which was such a strong tenet of his religion. Solomon abandoned the truth of his own divine wisdom: "Pride goes before destruction, and a haughty spirit before a fall. It is better to be of a lowly spirit and

among the poor than to divide the spoil with the proud"
(Prov. 16:18–19).

It was not tolerance, it was arrogance that caused
Solomon's eventual downfall. The aim of tolerance is not to
dilute our differences to the extent that we lose our unique
identities. Tolerance aims at allowing each of us to celebrate
our diversity within the context of our unity. The embrace of
diversity does not mean the diminishment of identity.
Solomon's openness to other religions could have enabled
him to become a better Jew. Solomon's openness to other
cultures could have made him more accountable for the
health of his own.

For a while in his career, this is precisely what happened,
and as a result Judaism was able to flourish in coexistence and
peace with other religions throughout the region. Then arrogance and avarice arose to contaminate the faith of Solomon
and to dismantle his noble network of interreligious dialogue, economic collaboration, and cultural exchange. This is
the charge and the challenge bequeathed to us through the
life and the leadership of Solomon. May his successes make
us wise; and may his failures make us wiser.

QUESTIONS FOR REFLECTION

1. What is the distinction between Christian witness and
   Christian proselytization?

2. What kinds of deep questions draw persons to houses
   of worship today?

3. How is the integrity of one's Christian witness affected
   when one's deeds are not in concert with one's creeds?

4. Why are the effects of one's faith more pertinent to
   one's evangelism than are the doctrines of one's faith?

5. Is the call for interfaith dialogue and religious tolerance
   tantamount to the dilution of one's own religious
   convictions?

notes

CHAPTER ONE
The First Key: Wisdom

1. Martin Luther King Jr, "Letter from the Birmingham Jail," in *Why Can't We Wait,* ed. Martin Luther King Jr. (New York: Harper & Row, 1964), 77–100. See also www .kingpapers.org.

2. Clay Evans, "I've Got a Testimony," *I've Got a Testimony* (compact disc) ©1997 by Meek Records.

3. J. Bennett Guess, "Does Jesus Love Wal-Mart's Low-Wage Workers? Justice and Witness Ministries Endorses 'Wal-Mart Week of Action,'" *UC News* 21/5 (October/November 2005), 10–11.

4. Ibid., 11.

CHAPTER TWO
The Second Key: Work

1. William Sloan Coffin, *The Heart Is a Little to the Left* (Hanover, N.H.: University Press of New England [for] Dartmouth College, 1999), 58.

2. Desmond Tutu, speaking at the 2006 Clinton Global Initiative Annual Meeting, September 21, 2006. See also www

.clintonglobalinitiative.org/NETCOMMUNITY/Document
.Doc?&id=88, page 28 of the transcript.

3. Joe Klein, "Let's Have an Antipoverty Caucus," *Time* (October 3, 2005), 29.

4. See www.globalsullivanprinciples.org and www.the sullivanfoundation.org.

CHAPTER THREE

The Third Key: Worship

1. Martin Luther King Jr, "The Three Dimensions of a Complete Life," sermon delivered at New Covenant Baptist Church, Chicago, Illinois, 9 April 1967. See also www.king papers.org.

2. John Shelby Spong, *Living in Sin?: A Bishop Rethinks Human Sexuality* (San Francisco: Harper & Row, 1988), 38.

3. William Sloan Coffin, *A Passion for the Possible: A Message to U.S. Churches* (Louisville: Westminster John Knox Press, 1993), 7–8.

4. Senator John F. Kennedy, speech to the Greater Houston Ministerial Association, Houston, Texas, 12 September 1960. In *Freedom of Communications,* final report of the Committee on Commerce, United States Senate, part 1, 208–9 (1961), Senate Rept. 87–994.

5. Jim Wallis, *God's Politics: Why the Right Gets It Wrong and the Left Doesn't Get It* (New York: HarperCollins, 2005), front flap copy.

6. Ibid.

7. Rev. Dr. Joseph E. Lowery, Jubilee Day sermon, Victory Church, Stone Mountain, Georgia, January 1, 2005.

CHAPTER FOUR

The Fourth Key: Witness

1. John Blake, "Honoring Many Paths: Some Say Religious Inclusivity Is Necessary in a Shrinking World, but Those

Who Practice It Sometimes Pay a Steep Price," *Atlanta Journal Constitution*, December 17, 2005, B1.

2. Charles Kimball, *When Religion Becomes Evil: Five Warning Signs* (San Francisco: HarperSanFrancisco, 2003).

3. Bruce Feiler, *Abraham: A Journey to the Heart of Three Faiths* (New York: William Morrow, 2002).

Made in the USA
Las Vegas, NV
22 March 2022